Presented
to

_____

by

_____

_____
Date

_____
Occasion

DEDICATION

❖

I dedicate this Minister's Topical Bible to my own Father, Dr. J. E. Murdock, under whose mentorship I received a passion for obedience and being led by the Spirit.

"Daddy, you left me the greatest legacy a father can leave a son. Memories...of your insatiable pursuit of the Presence of God.

Our family altars, prayer times, every morning and every night with us 7 children are forever engraved in my mind and my heart. You are a Treasure to me.

I have never heard you curse... never seen a cigarette between your lips...never seen a liquor bottle in your hand...never heard you lie.

I am grateful to you for making holy living your goal."

From A Very Thankful Son,

Mike

TABLE OF CONTENTS

Unless otherwise indicated, all scripture quotations are taken from the King James Version of the Bible.
The Minister's Topical Bible
ISBN 1-56394-148-1/B-32
Copyright © 1988 by **MIKE MURDOCK**
All publishing rights belong exclusively to Wisdom International
Publisher/Editor: Deborah Murdock Johnson
Published by The Wisdom Center
P. O. Box 99 · Denton, Texas 76202
1-888-WISDOM-1 (1-888-947-3661)
Website: **thewisdomcenter.tv**

YOUR RELATIONSHIP TO GOD

❦ 1 ❦

YOUR DAILY PRAYER LIFE

But thou, when thou prayest, enter into thy closet, and when thou hast shut thy door, pray to thy Father which is in secret; and thy Father which seeth in secret shall reward thee openly.

But when ye pray, use not vain repetitions, as the heathen do: for they think that they shall be heard for their much speaking.   *Matthew 6:6,7*

Ask, and it shall be given you; seek, and ye shall find; knock, and it shall be opened unto you:

For every one that asketh receiveth; and he that seeketh findeth; and to him that knocketh it shall be opened.

Or what man is there of you, whom if his son ask bread, will he give him a stone?   *Matthew 7:7-9*

And all things, whatsoever ye shall ask in prayer, believing, ye shall receive.   *Matthew 21:22*

Watch and pray, that ye enter not into temptation: the spirit indeed is willing, but the flesh is weak.

Matthew 26:41

And in the morning, rising up a great while before day, He went out, and departed into a solitary place, and there prayed.   *Mark 1:35*

Therefore I say unto you, What things soever ye desire, when ye pray, believe that ye receive them, and ye shall have them.   *Mark 11:24*

Bless them that curse you, and pray for them which despitefully use you. *Luke 6:28*

And He spake a parable unto them to this end, that men ought always to pray, and not to faint; *Luke 18:1*

Likewise the Spirit also helpeth our infirmities: for we know not what we should pray for as we ought: but the Spirit itself maketh intercession for us with groanings which cannot be uttered. *Romans 8:26*

Elias was a man subject to like passions as we are, and he prayed earnestly that it might not rain: and it rained not on the earth by the space of three years and six months. *James 5:17*

But ye, beloved, building up yourselves on your most holy faith, praying in the Holy Ghost,... *Jude 1:20*

≈ 2 ≈

YOUR DAILY BIBLE STUDY

This book of the law shall not depart out of thy mouth; but thou shalt meditate therein day and night, that thou mayest observe to do according to all that is written therein: for then thou shalt make thy way prosperous, and then thou shalt have good success.

Joshua 1:8

But his delight is in the law of the Lord; and in His law doth he meditate day and night.   *Psalm 1:2*

The law of the Lord is perfect, converting the soul: the testimony of the Lord is sure, making wise the simple.   *Psalm 19:7*

Thy Word have I hid in mine heart,

that I might not sin against Thee.

Psalm 119:11

Therefore whosoever heareth these sayings of Mine, and doeth them, I will liken him unto a wise man, which built his house upon a rock:

Matthew 7:24

Search the scriptures; for in them ye think ye have eternal life: and they are they which testify of Me. *John 5:39*

Then said Jesus to those Jews which believed on Him, If ye continue in My Word, then are ye My disciples indeed; *John 8:31*

Study to shew thyself approved unto God, a workman that needeth not to be ashamed, rightly dividing the Word of truth. *2 Timothy 2:15*

All scripture is given by inspiration of God, and is profitable for doctrine, for reproof, for correction, for instruction in righteousness:

2 Timothy 3:16

❧ 3 ❧

YOUR ATTITUDE TOWARD PRAISE AND WORSHIP

Sing unto the Lord, all the earth; shew forth from day to day His salvation.

Declare His glory among the heathen; His marvellous works among all nations.   *1 Chronicles 16:23,24*

Give unto the Lord the glory due unto His name: bring an offering, and come before Him: worship the Lord in the beauty of holiness.

1 Chronicles 16:29

It came even to pass, as the trumpeters and singers were as one, to make one sound to be heard in praising and thanking the Lord; and when they lifted up their voice with the trumpets and cymbals and instruments of musick, and praised the Lord, saying, For He is good; for His mercy endureth for ever: that then the house was filled with a cloud, even the house of the Lord;   *2 Chronicles 5:13*

And they sang together by course in praising and giving thanks unto the Lord; because He is good, for His mercy endureth for ever toward Israel. And all the people shouted with a great shout, when they praised the Lord, because the foundation of the house of the Lord was laid.   *Ezra 3:11*

I will give Thee thanks in the great congregation: I will praise Thee among much people.   *Psalm 35:18*

Serve the Lord with gladness: come before His presence with singing.
Psalm 100:2

Thy statutes have been my songs in the house of my pilgrimage.
Psalm 119:54

Giving thanks always for all things unto God and the Father in the name of our Lord Jesus Christ;   *Ephesians 5:20*

Be careful for nothing; but in every thing by prayer and supplication with thanksgiving let your requests be made known unto God.   *Philippians 4:6*

In every thing give thanks: for this is the will of God in Christ Jesus concerning you.   *1 Thessalonians 5:18*

By Him therefore let us offer the sacrifice of praise to God continually, that is, the fruit of our lips giving thanks to His name.   *Hebrews 13:15*

Saying with a loud voice, Worthy is the Lamb that was slain to receive power, and riches, and wisdom, and strength, and honour, and glory, and blessing.   *Revelation 5:12*

4

DEVELOPING HOURLY
OBEDIENCE TO
GOD'S VOICE

And it shall come to pass, if thou shalt hearken diligently unto the voice of the Lord thy God, to observe and to do all His commandments which I command thee this day, that the Lord thy God will set thee on high above all nations of the earth:

And all these blessings shall come on thee, and overtake thee, if thou shalt hearken unto the voice of the Lord thy God. *Deuteronomy 28:1,2*

And Samuel said, Hath the Lord as great delight in burnt offerings and sacrifices, as in obeying the voice of the Lord? Behold, to obey is better than sacrifice, and to hearken than the fat of rams. *1 Samuel 15:22*

Learn to do well; seek judgment, relieve the oppressed, judge the fatherless, plead for the widow.

Come now, and let us reason together, saith the Lord: though your sins be as scarlet, they shall be as white as snow; though they be red like crimson, they shall be as wool.

If ye be willing and obedient, ye shall eat the good of the land:
Isaiah 1:17-19

For as by one man's disobedience many were made sinners, so by the obedience of one shall many be made righteous. *Romans 5:19*

For as many as are led by the Spirit of God, they are the sons of God.
Romans 8:14

Therefore to him that knoweth to do good, and doeth it not, to him it is sin. *1 Peter 4:17*

If we say that we have fellowship with Him, and walk in darkness, we lie, and do not the truth: *1 John 1:6*

And hereby we do know that we know Him, if we keep His commandments.
He that saith, I know Him, and keepeth not His commandments, is a liar, and the truth is not in him.
But whoso keepeth His word, in him verily is the love of God perfected: hereby know we that we are in Him.
1 John 2:3-5

And whatsoever we ask, we receive of Him, because we keep His commandments, and do those things that are pleasing in His sight.   *1 John 3:22*

And this is love, that we walk after His commandments.   This is the commandment, That, as ye have heard from the beginning, ye should walk in it.   *2 John 1:6*

One Hour
    In The Presence Of God
Will Reveal Any Flaw
    In Your Most Carefully
Laid Plan.

-MIKE MURDOCK

YOUR SPIRITUAL LIFE

~ 5 ~

WHEN YOU NEED FRESH MOTIVATION

For the needy shall not alway be forgotten: the expectation of the poor shall not perish for ever.   *Psalm 9:18*

Be of good courage, and He shall strengthen your heart, all ye that hope in the Lord.   *Psalm 31:24*

Behold, the eye of the Lord is upon them that fear Him, upon them that hope in His mercy;   *Psalm 33:18*

For in Thee, O Lord, do I hope: Thou wilt hear, O Lord my God.

Psalm 38:15

Why art thou cast down, O my soul? and why art thou disquieted within me? hope in God: for I shall yet praise Him, Who is the health of my countenance, and my God.   *Psalm 43:5*

But I will hope continually, and will yet praise Thee more and more.

Psalm 71:14

Hope deferred maketh the heart sick: but when the desire cometh, it is a tree of life.   *Proverbs 13:12*

Who against hope believed in hope, that he might become the father of many nations, according to that which was spoken, So shall thy seed be.

Romans 4:18

There hath no temptation taken you but such as is common to man: but God is faithful, Who will not suffer you

to be tempted above that ye are able;
but will with the temptation also make
a way to escape, that ye may be able to
bear it.   *1 Corinthians 10:13*

And God is able to make all grace
abound toward you; that ye, always
having all sufficiency in all things, may
abound to every good work:
                        2 Corinthians 9:8

That He would grant you,
according to the riches of His glory, to
be strengthened with might by His
Spirit in the inner man;*Ephesians 3:16*

Put on the whole armour of God,
that ye may be able to stand against the
wiles of the devil.   *Ephesians 6:11*

Praying always with all prayer
and supplication in the Spirit, and
watching thereunto with all perseverance and supplication for all saints;
                        Ephesians 6:18

And the peace of God, which

passeth all understanding, shall keep your hearts and minds through Christ Jesus.

Finally, brethren, whatsoever things are true, whatsoever things are honest, whatsoever things are just, whatsoever things are pure, whatsoever things are lovely, whatsoever things are of good report; if there be any virtue, and if there be any praise, think on these things. *Philippians 4:7,8*

But my God shall supply all your need according to His riches in glory by Christ Jesus. *Philippians 4:19*

Wherefore gird up the loins of your mind, be sober, and hope to the end for the grace that is to be brought unto you at the revelation of Jesus Christ;
1 Peter 1:13

Be sober, be vigilant; because your adversary the devil, as a roaring lion, walketh about, seeking whom he may devour: *1 Peter 5:8*

6

WHEN YOU NEED YOUR FAITH STRENGTHENED

Wherefore, if God so clothe the grass of the field, which to day is, and to morrow is cast into the oven, shall He not much more clothe you, O ye of little faith?   *Matthew 6:30*

And He saith unto them, Why are ye fearful, O ye of little faith? Then He arose, and rebuked the winds and the sea; and there was a great calm.
Matthew 8:26

And Jesus said unto them, Because of your unbelief: for verily I say unto you, If ye have faith as a grain of mustard seed, ye shall say unto this mountain, Remove hence to yonder place; and it shall remove; and nothing shall be impossible unto you.

Matthew 17:20

Jesus answered and said unto them, Verily I say unto you, If ye have faith, and doubt not, ye shall not only do this which is done to the fig tree, but also if ye shall say unto this mountain, Be thou removed, and be thou cast into the sea; it shall be done.

Matthew 21:21

But I have prayed for thee, that thy faith fail not: and when thou art converted, strengthen thy brethren.

Luke 22:32

So then faith cometh by hearing, and hearing by the word of God.

Romans 10:17

For we walk by faith, not by sight:

2 Corinthians 5:7

Above all, taking the shield of faith, wherewith ye shall be able to

quench all the fiery darts of the wicked.
Ephesians 6:16

But let us, who are of the day, be sober, putting on the breastplate of faith and love; and for an helmet, the hope of salvation.   *1 Thessalonians 5:8*

Now the just shall live by faith: but if any man draw back, my soul shall have no pleasure in him.
Hebrews 10:38

Now faith is the substance of things hoped for, the evidence of things not seen.   *Hebrews 11:1*

But without faith it is impossible to please Him: for he that cometh to God must believe that He is, and that He is a rewarder of them that diligently seek Him.   *Hebrews 11:6*

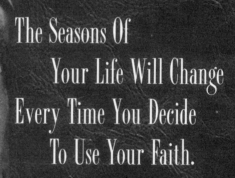

The Seasons Of
Your Life Will Change
Every Time You Decide
To Use Your Faith.

-MIKE MURDOCK

⚘ 7 ⚘

WHEN YOU NEED
SPECIAL WISDOM IN
DECISION-MAKING

I will bless the Lord, Who hath given me counsel: my reins also instruct me in the night seasons.

Psalm 16:7

The entrance of Thy words giveth light; it giveth understanding unto the simple. *Psalm 119:130*

For the Lord giveth wisdom: out of His mouth cometh knowledge and understanding. *Proverbs 2:6*

Trust in the Lord with all thine heart; and lean not unto thine own understanding. *Proverbs 3:5*

And thine ears shall hear a word behind thee, saying, This is the way, walk ye in it, when ye turn to the right hand, and when ye turn to the left.

Isaiah 30:21

For I will give you a mouth and wisdom, which all your adversaries shall not be able to gainsay nor resist.

Luke 21:15

Howbeit when He, the Spirit of truth, is come, He will guide you into all truth: for He shall not speak of Himself; but whatsoever He shall hear, that shall He speak: and He will shew you things to come. *John 16:13*

For as many as are led by the Spirit of God, they are the sons of God.

Romans 8:14

That the God of our Lord Jesus Christ, the Father of glory, may give unto you the spirit of wisdom and revelation in the knowledge of Him:

Ephesians 1:17

The eyes of your understanding being enlightened; that ye may know what is the hope of His calling, and what the riches of the glory of His inheritance in the saints,

Ephesians 1:18

For this cause we also, since the day we heard it, do not cease to pray for you, and to desire that ye might be filled with the knowledge of His will in all wisdom and spiritual understanding;

Colossians 1:9

If any of you lack wisdom, let him ask of God, that giveth to all men liberally, and upbraideth not; and it shall be given him.

James 1:5

But the wisdom that is from above is first pure, then peaceable, gentle, and easy to be intreated, full of mercy and good fruits, without partiality, and without hypocrisy.

James 3:17

8

WHEN YOU NEED TO MASTER A PERSONAL PROBLEM

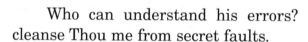

Who can understand his errors? cleanse Thou me from secret faults.

Psalm 19:12

Remember not the sins of my youth, nor my transgressions: according to Thy mercy remember Thou me for Thy goodness' sake, O Lord.

For Thy name's sake, O Lord, pardon mine iniquity; for it is great.

Psalm 25:7,11

Though he fall, he shall not be utterly cast down: for the Lord upholdeth him with His hand.

Psalm 37:24

Create in me a clean heart, O God;
and renew a right spirit within me.
Psalm 51:10

As far as the east is from the west,
so far hath He removed our transgressions from us.   *Psalm 103:12*

I, even I, am He that blotteth out
thy transgressions for Mine own sake,
and will not remember thy sins.
Isaiah 43:25

Likewise the Spirit also helpeth
our infirmities: for we know not what
we should pray for as we ought: but the
Spirit itself maketh intercession for us
with groanings which cannot be
uttered.   *Romans 8:26*

Let us therefore come boldly unto
the throne of grace, that we may obtain
mercy, and find grace to help in time of
need.   *Hebrews 4:16*

If we confess our sins, He is
faithful and just to forgive us our sins,
and to cleanse us from all unrighteous-
ness.   *1 John 1:9*

You Cannot Change
What You Are Unwilling
To Confront.

-MIKE MURDOCK

❧ 9 ❧

When You Need To Conquer Worry

I will both lay me down in peace, and sleep: for Thou, Lord, only makest me dwell in safety. *Psalm 4:8*

Delight thyself also in the Lord: and He shall give thee the desires of thine heart. *Psalm 37:4*

In God I will praise His word, in God I have put my trust; I will not fear what flesh can do unto me. *Psalm 56:4*

Great peace have they which love Thy law: and nothing shall offend them. *Psalm 119:165*

Behold, God is my salvation; I will trust, and not be afraid: for the Lord Jehovah is my strength and my song;

He also is become my salvation.

Isaiah 12:2

Thou wilt keep Him in perfect peace, whose mind is stayed on Thee: because He trusteth in Thee.

Isaiah 26:3

So shall they fear the name of the Lord from the west, and His glory from the rising of the sun. When the enemy shall come in like a flood, the Spirit of the Lord shall lift up a standard against him. *Isaiah 59:19*

Peace I leave with you, My peace I give unto you: not as the world giveth, give I unto you. Let not your heart be troubled, neither let it be afraid.

John 14:27

For to be carnally minded is death; but to be spiritually minded is life and peace. *Romans 8:6*

And let the peace of God rule in your hearts, to the which also ye are called in one body; and be ye thankful.

Colossians 3:15

The Difference
Between Seasons Is
A Friendship.

-MIKE MURDOCK

～ 10 ～

WHEN YOU NEED A TRUSTWORTHY FRIEND

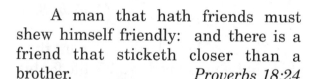

A man that hath friends must shew himself friendly: and there is a friend that sticketh closer than a brother. *Proverbs 18:24*

Two are better than one; because they have a good reward for their labour.

For if they fall, the one will lift up his fellow: but woe to him that is alone when he falleth; for he hath not another to help him up.

And if one prevail against him, two shall withstand him; and a threefold cord is not quickly broken.

Ecclesiastes 4:9,10,12

Can two walk together, except they
be agreed?   *Amos 3:3*

Then they that feared the Lord
spake often one to another: and the
Lord hearkened, and heard it, and a
book of remembrance was written
before Him for them that feared the
Lord, and that thought upon His name.
Malachi 3:16

Greater love hath no man than
this, that a man lay down his life for his
friends.   *John 15:13*

But if we walk in the light, as He is
in the light, we have fellowship one
with another, and the blood of Jesus
Christ His Son cleanseth us from all
sin.   *1 John 1:7*

11

WHEN YOU NEED DIVINE REASSURANCE

What is man, that Thou art mindful of him? and the son of man, that Thou visitest him?

For Thou hast made him a little lower than the angels, and hast crowned him with glory and honour.
Psalm 8:4,5

Rejoice, and be exceeding glad: for great is your reward in heaven: for so persecuted they the prophets which were before you. *Matthew 5:12*

Nay, in all these things we are more than conquerors through Him that loved us. *Romans 8:37*

QUALITIES OF AN UNCOMMON SHEPHERD

～ 12 ～

COMPASSION

Thou shalt not see thy brother's ox or his sheep go astray, and hide thyself from them: thou shalt in any case bring them again unto thy brother.

Deuteronomy 22:1

A good man sheweth favour, and lendeth: he will guide his affairs with discretion. *Psalm 112:5*

But when He saw the multitudes, He was moved with compassion on them, because they fainted, and were scattered abroad, as sheep having no shepherd. *Matthew 9:36*

But a certain Samaritan, as He journeyed, came where He was: and when He saw him, He had compassion on him,
And went to him, and bound up his wounds, pouring in oil and wine, and set him on his own beast, and brought him to an inn, and took care of him.
Luke 10:33,34

We then that are strong ought to bear the infirmities of the weak, and not to please ourselves. *Romans 15:1*

Pure religion and undefiled before God and the Father is this, To visit the fatherless and widows in their affliction, and to keep himself unspotted from the world. *James 1:27*

But whoso hath this world's good, and seeth his brother have need, and shutteth up his bowels of compassion from him, how dwelleth the love of God in him? *1 John 3:17*

Your Passion Determines
Your Courage.

-MIKE MURDOCK

❧ 13 ❧

COURAGE

The wicked flee when no man pursueth: but the righteous are bold as a lion. *Proverbs 28:1*

He that rebuketh a man afterwards shall find more favour than he that flattereth with the tongue.
Proverbs 28:23

It is better to hear the rebuke of the wise, than for a man to hear the song of fools. *Ecclesiastes 7:5*

Now when they saw the boldness of Peter and John, and perceived that they were unlearned and ignorant men, they marvelled; and they took knowledge of them, that they had been with Jesus.

And now, Lord, behold their threatenings: and grant unto Thy servants, that with all boldness they may speak Thy word,

And when they had prayed, the place was shaken where they were assembled together; and they were all filled with the Holy Ghost, and they spake the word of God with boldness.

Acts 4:13,29,31

Watch ye, stand fast in the faith, quit you like men, be strong.

1 Corinthians 16:13

And have no fellowship with the unfruitful works of darkness, but rather reprove them.   *Ephesians 5:11*

And for me, that utterance may be given unto me, that I may open my mouth boldly, to make known the mystery of the gospel,   *Ephesians 6:19*

And many of the brethren in the Lord, waxing confident by my bonds, are much more bold to speak the word without fear.   *Philippians 1:14*

Only let your conversation be as it becometh the gospel of Christ: that whether I come and see you, or else be absent, I may hear of your affairs, that ye stand fast in one spirit, with one mind striving together for the faith of the gospel;

And in nothing terrified by your adversaries: which is to them an evident token of perdition, but to you of salvation, and that of God.

Philippians 1:27,28

For God hath not given us the spirit of fear; but of power, and of love, and of a sound mind.   *2 Timothy 1:7*

The Magnetism Of Kindness
Always Outlasts
The Memory Of Genius.

-MIKE MURDOCK

≈ 14 ≈

DIPLOMACY

He that is slow to wrath is of great understanding: but he that is hasty of spirit exalteth folly.   *Proverbs 14:29*

A soft answer turneth away wrath: but grievous words stir up anger.
Proverbs 15:1

A wrathful man stirreth up strife: but he that is slow to anger appeaseth strife.   *Proverbs 15:18*

He that is slow to anger is better than the mighty; and he that ruleth his spirit than he that taketh a city.
Proverbs 16:32

By long forbearing is a prince persuaded, and a soft tongue breaketh the bone.   *Proverbs 25:15*

Blessed are the peacemakers: for they shall be called the children of God.
Matthew 5:9

And the servant of the Lord must not strive; but be gentle unto all men, apt to teach, patient,

In meekness instructing those that oppose themselves; if God peradventure will give them repentance to the acknowledging of the truth;

And that they may recover themselves out of the snare of the devil, who are taken captive by him at his will.
2 Timothy 2:24-26

Put them in mind to be subject to principalities and powers, to obey magistrates, to be ready to every good work,

To speak evil of no man, to be no brawlers, but gentle, shewing all meekness unto all men.
Titus 3:1,2

But the wisdom that is from above is first pure, then peaceable, gentle, and easy to be intreated, full of mercy and good fruits, without partiality, and without hypocrisy.
James 3:17

✑ 15 ✑

DISCIPLINE

And Moses said unto them, Stand still, and I will hear what the Lord will command concerning you. *Numbers 9:8*

Stand in awe, and sin not: commune with your own heart upon your bed, and be still. *Psalm 4:4*

Judge me, O Lord; for I have walked in mine integrity: I have trusted also in the Lord; therefore I shall not slide. *Psalm 26:1*

But as for me, I will walk in mine integrity: redeem me, and be merciful unto me. *Psalm 26:11*

Be still, and know that I am God: I will be exalted among the heathen, I

will be exalted in the earth.
Psalm 46:10

For their heart was not right with Him, neither were they stedfast in His covenant. *Psalm 78:37*

He will not suffer thy foot to be moved: He that keepeth thee will not slumber. *Psalm 121:3*

Then shalt thou walk in thy way safely, and thy foot shall not stumble.
For the Lord shall be thy confidence, and shall keep thy foot from being taken. *Proverbs 3:23,26*

For though I be absent in the flesh, yet am I with you in the spirit, joying and beholding your order, and the stedfastness of your faith in Christ.
Colossians 2:5

Let us hold fast the profession of our faith without wavering; (for He is faithful that promised;) *Hebrews 10:23*

Be not carried about with divers
and strange doctrines. For it is a good
thing that the heart be established with
grace; not with meats, which have not
profited them that have been occupied
therein. *Hebrews 13:9*

Be ye also patient; stablish your
hearts: for the coming of the Lord
draweth nigh. *James 5:8*

Be sober, be vigilant; because your
adversary the devil, as a roaring lion,
walketh about, seeking whom he may
devour:
Whom resist stedfast in the faith,
knowing that the same afflictions are
accomplished in your brethren that are
in the world. *1 Peter 5:8,9*

～ 16 ～

ENTHUSIASM

For they all made us afraid, saying, Their hands shall be weakened from the work, that it be not done. Now therefore, O God, strengthen my hands.
Nehemiah 6:9

Be of good courage, and He shall strengthen your heart, all ye that hope in the Lord.   *Psalm 31:24*

My soul melteth for heaviness: strengthen thou me according unto Thy Word.   *Psalm 119:28*

For thus saith the Lord God, the Holy One of Israel; In returning and rest shall ye be saved; in quietness and in confidence shall be your strength: and ye would not.   *Isaiah 30:15*

He giveth power to the faint; and

to them that have no might He increaseth strength.

Even the youths shall faint and be weary, and the young men shall utterly fall:

But they that wait upon the Lord shall renew their strength; they shall mount up with wings as eagles; they shall run, and not be weary; and they shall walk, and not faint.

Isaiah 40:29-31

Fear thou not; for I am with thee: be not dismayed; for I am thy God: I will strengthen thee; yea, I will help thee; yea, I will uphold thee with the right hand of My righteousness.

Isaiah 41:10

The Lord God is my strength, and He will make my feet like hinds' feet, and He will make me to walk upon mine high places.   *Habakkuk 3:19*

Strengthened with all might, according to His glorious power, unto all patience and longsuffering with joyfulness;   *Colossians 1:11*

What You Are
You Create
Around You.

-MIKE MURDOCK

❧ 17 ❧

EXAMPLE

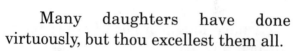

Many daughters have done virtuously, but thou excellest them all.
Proverbs 31:29

Forasmuch as an excellent spirit, and knowledge, and understanding, interpreting of dreams, and shewing of hard sentences, and dissolving of doubts, were found in the same Daniel, whom the king named Belteshazzar: now let Daniel be called, and he will shew the interpretation.   *Daniel 5:12*

Then this Daniel was preferred above the presidents and princes, because an excellent spirit was in him; and the king thought to set him over the whole realm.   *Daniel 6:3*

For I have given you an example, that ye should do as I have done to you.
John 13:15

Let no man despise thy youth; but be thou an example of the believers, in word, in conversation, in charity, in spirit, in faith, in purity. *1 Timothy 4:12*

I have fought a good fight, I have finished my course, I have kept the faith: *2 Timothy 4:7*

For even hereunto were ye called: because Christ also suffered for us, leaving us an example, that ye should follow His steps: *1 Peter 2:21*

According as His divine power hath given unto us all things that pertain unto life and godliness, through the knowledge of Him that hath called us to glory and virtue:
For if these things be in you, and abound, they make you that ye shall neither be barren nor unfruitful in the knowledge of our Lord Jesus Christ.
2 Peter 1:3,8

18

HUMILITY

The meek will He guide in judgment: and the meek will He teach His way.   *Psalm 25:9*

Surely He scorneth the scorners: but He giveth grace unto the lowly.
                    Proverbs 3:34

When pride cometh, then cometh shame: but with the lowly is wisdom.
                    Proverbs 11:2

Better it is to be of an humble spirit with the lowly, than to divide the spoil with the proud.   *Proverbs 16:19*

By humility and the fear of the Lord are riches, and honour, and life.
                    Proverbs 22:4

For thus saith the high and lofty One that inhabiteth eternity, Whose name is Holy; I dwell in the high and holy place, with him also that is of a contrite and humble spirit, to revive the spirit of the humble, and to revive the heart of the contrite ones. *Isaiah 57:15*

And Jesus called a little child unto Him, and set him in the midst of them,

And said, Verily I say unto you, Except ye be converted, and become as little children, ye shall not enter into the kingdom of heaven.

Whosoever therefore shall humble himself as this little child, the same is greatest in the kingdom of heaven.

Matthew 18:2-4

And whosoever shall exalt himself shall be abased; and he that shall humble himself shall be exalted.

Matthew 23:12

Let nothing be done through strife or vainglory; but in lowliness of mind let each esteem other better than themselves. *Philippians 2:3*

But He giveth more grace. Wherefore he saith, God resisteth the proud, but giveth grace unto the humble.

Humble yourselves in the sight of the Lord, and He shall lift you up.

James 4:6,10

Likewise, ye younger, submit yourselves unto the elder. Yea, all of you be subject one to another, and be clothed with humility: for God resisteth the proud, and giveth grace to the humble.

Humble yourselves therefore under the mighty hand of God, that He may exalt you in due time: *1 Peter 5:5,6*

≈ **19** ≈

KINDNESS

Blessed are the merciful: for they shall obtain mercy.   *Matthew 5:7*

But love ye your enemies, and do good, and lend, hoping for nothing again; and your reward shall be great, and ye shall be the children of the Highest: *Luke 6:35*

Now the God of patience and consolation grant you to be likeminded one toward another,   *Romans 15:5*

Brethren, if a man be overtaken in a fault, ye which are spiritual, restore such an one in the spirit of meekness; considering thyself, lest thou also be tempted.   *Galatians 6:1*

～ 20 ～

LISTENING

And he read therein before the street that was before the water gate from the morning until midday, before the men and the women, and those that could understand; and the ears of all the people were attentive unto the book of the law. *Nehemiah 8:3*

Bless the Lord, ye His angels, that excel in strength, that do His commandments, hearkening unto the voice of His word. *Psalm 103:20*

But whoso hearkeneth unto Me shall dwell safely, and shall be quiet from fear of evil. *Proverbs 1:33*

Hear, ye children, the instruction of a father, and attend to know understanding.

My son, attend to my words; incline thine ear unto my sayings.

Proverbs 4:1,20

Hear instruction, and be wise, and refuse it not.

Blessed is the man that heareth Me, watching daily at My gates, waiting at the posts of My doors.

Proverbs 8:33,34

The ear that heareth the reproof of life abideth among the wise.

Proverbs 15:31

He that answereth a matter before he heareth it, it is folly and shame unto him. *Proverbs 18:13*

So then faith cometh by hearing, and hearing by the word of God.

Romans 10:17

Wherefore, my beloved brethren, let every man be swift to hear, slow to speak, slow to wrath: *James 1:19*

If any man have an ear, let him hear. *Revelation 13:9*

21

PATIENCE

Be ye strong therefore, and let not your hands be weak: for your work shall be rewarded.   *2 Chronicles 15:7*

Why art thou cast down, O my soul? and why art thou disquieted within me? hope in God: for I shall yet praise Him, Who is the health of my countenance, and my God.   *Psalm 43:5*

For Thou art my hope, O Lord God: Thou art my trust from my youth.
Psalm 71:5

But they that wait upon the Lord shall renew their strength; they shall mount up with wings as eagles; they shall run, and not be weary; and they shall walk, and not faint.   *Isaiah 40:31*

Blessed is the man that trusteth in the Lord, and whose hope the Lord is.

For he shall be as a tree planted by the waters, and that spreadeth out her roots by the river, and shall not see when heat cometh, but her leaf shall be green; and shall not be careful in the year of drought, neither shall cease from yielding fruit.   *Jeremiah 17:7,8*

But that on the good ground are they, which in an honest and good heart, having heard the word, keep it, and bring forth fruit with patience.

Luke 8:15

Cast not away therefore your confidence, which hath great recompence of reward.   *Hebrews 10:35*

Knowing this, that the trying of your faith worketh patience.

But let patience have her perfect work, that ye may be perfect and entire, wanting nothing.   *James 1:3,4*

☙ 22 ☙

PERSISTENCE

My heart is fixed, O God, my heart is fixed: I will sing and give praise.

Psalm 57:7

Then the king commanded, and they brought Daniel, and cast him into the den of lions. Now the king spake and said unto Daniel, Thy God whom thou servest continually, He will deliver thee.

And when he came to the den, he cried with a lamentable voice unto Daniel: and the king spake and said to Daniel, O Daniel, servant of the living God, is thy God, Whom thou servest continually, able to deliver thee from the lions? *Daniel 6:16,20*

And Jesus said unto him, No man,

having put his hand to the plough, and looking back, is fit for the kingdom of God. *Luke 9:62*

Then said Jesus to those Jews which believed on Him, If ye continue in My word, then are ye My disciples indeed; *John 8:31*

As the Father hath loved Me, so have I loved you: continue ye in My love. *John 15:9*

But we will give ourselves continually to prayer, and to the ministry of the word. *Acts 6:4*

Let that therefore abide in you, which ye have heard from the beginning. If that which ye have heard from the beginning shall remain in you, ye also shall continue in the Son, and in the Father. *1 John 2:24*

~ 23 ~

PREPARATION

He becometh poor that dealeth
with a slack hand: but the hand of the
diligent maketh rich.

He that gathereth in summer is a
wise son: but he that sleepeth in
harvest is a son that causeth shame.

Proverbs 10:4,5

Seest thou a man diligent in his
business? he shall stand before kings;
he shall not stand before mean men.

Proverbs 22:29

And the Lord answered me, and
said, Write the vision, and make it plain
upon tables, that he may run that
readeth it.   *Habakkuk 2:2*

Therefore whosoever heareth
these sayings of Mine, and doeth them,
I will liken him unto a wise man, which

built his house upon a rock:

And the rain descended, and the floods came, and the winds blew, and beat upon that house; and it fell not: for it was founded upon a rock.

And every one that heareth these sayings of mine, and doeth them not, shall be likened unto a foolish man, which built his house upon the sand:

And the rain descended, and the floods came, and the winds blew, and beat upon that house; and it fell: and great was the fall of it.

Matthew 7:24-27

For which of you, intending to build a tower, sitteth not down first, and counteth the cost, whether he have sufficient to finish it? *Luke 14:28*

Study to shew thyself approved unto God, a workman that needeth not to be ashamed, rightly dividing the word of truth. *2 Timothy 2:15*

If any of you lack wisdom, let him ask of God, that giveth to all men liberally, and upbraideth not; and it shall be given him. *James 1:5*

24

SERVANT'S HEART

Withhold not good from them to whom it is due, when it is in the power of thine hand to do it.   *Proverbs 3:27*

If thine enemy be hungry, give him bread to eat; and if he be thirsty, give him water to drink: *Proverbs 25:21*

And if thou draw out thy soul to the hungry, and satisfy the afflicted soul; then shall thy light rise in obscurity, and thy darkness be as the noon day:

And the Lord shall guide thee continually, and satisfy thy soul in drought, and make fat thy bones: and thou shalt be like a watered garden, and like a spring of water, whose waters fail not.   *Isaiah 58:10,11*

And whosoever shall give to drink unto one of these little ones a cup of cold water only in the name of a disciple, verily I say unto you, he shall in no wise lose his reward.

Matthew 10:42

For I was an hungered, and ye gave Me meat: I was thirsty, and ye gave Me drink: I was a stranger, and ye took Me in:

Naked, and ye clothed Me: I was sick, and ye visited Me: I was in prison, and ye came unto Me.

And the King shall answer and say unto them, Verily I say unto you, Inasmuch as ye have done it unto one of the least of these my brethren, ye have done it unto Me. *Matthew 25:35,36,40*

The Attitude
        Of The Servant
Determines
        The Atmosphere
Of The Palace.

-MIKE MURDOCK

25

SINCERITY

That which is altogether just shalt thou follow, that thou mayest live, and inherit the land which the Lord thy God giveth thee. *Deuteronomy 16:20*

But thou shalt have a perfect and just weight, a perfect and just measure shalt thou have: that thy days may be lengthened in the land which the Lord thy God giveth thee.

Deuteronomy 25:15

Let thine eyes look right on, and let thine eyelids look straight before thee. *Proverbs 4:25*

A false balance is abomination to the Lord: but a just weight is His delight. *Proverbs 11:1*

Lying lips are abomination to the Lord: but they that deal truly are His delight. *Proverbs 12:22*

He that walketh righteously, and speaketh uprightly; he that despiseth the gain of oppressions, that shaketh his hands from holding of bribes, that stoppeth his ears from hearing of blood, and shutteth his eyes from seeing evil;
Isaiah 33:15

And herein do I exercise myself, to have always a conscience void of offence toward God, and toward men.
Acts 24:16

Providing for honest things, not only in the sight of the Lord, but also in the sight of men. *2 Corinthians 8:21*

Seeing ye have purified your souls in obeying the truth through the Spirit unto unfeigned love of the brethren, see that ye love one another with a pure heart fervently:
Being born again, not of corruptible seed, but of incorruptible, by the word of God, which liveth and abideth for ever. *1 Peter 1:22,23*

❧ 26 ❧

SPIRIT-FILLED

Lead me in Thy truth, and teach me: for Thou art the God of my salvation; on Thee do I wait all the day.

The meek will He guide in judgment: and the meek will He teach His way.

What man is he that feareth the Lord? him shall He teach in the way that He shall choose.   *Psalm 25:5,9,12*

But if thine eye be evil, thy whole body shall be full of darkness.   If therefore the light that is in thee be darkness, how great is that darkness!
Matthew 6:23

For the Holy Ghost shall teach you in the same hour what ye ought to say.
Luke 12:12

But the Comforter, which is the Holy Ghost, whom the Father will send in My name, He shall teach you all things, and bring all things to your remembrance, whatsoever I have said unto you. *John 14:26*

Howbeit when He, the Spirit of truth, is come, He will guide you into all truth: for He shall not speak of Himself; but whatsoever He shall hear, that shall He speak: and He will shew you things to come.

He shall glorify Me: for He shall receive of Mine, and shall shew it unto you. *John 16:13,14*

For as many as are led by the Spirit of God, they are the sons of God. *Romans 8:14*

For this cause we also, since the day we heard it, do not cease to pray for you, and to desire that ye might be filled with the knowledge of His will in all wisdom and spiritual understanding; *Colossians 1:9*

The Gift Of Truth Is
Only Celebrated
By The Seeker Of Truth.

-MIKE MURDOCK

27

TRUTHFUL

Lying lips are abomination to the Lord: but they that deal truly are His delight.   *Proverbs 12:22*

A true witness delivereth souls: but a deceitful witness speaketh lies.
                    Proverbs 14:25

Thus speaketh the Lord of hosts, saying, Execute true judgment, and shew mercy and compassions every man to his brother: *Zechariah 7:9*

I say the truth in Christ, I lie not, my conscience also bearing me witness in the Holy Ghost,   *Romans 9:1*

But speaking the truth in love, may grow up into Him in all things, which is the head, even Christ: *Ephesians 4:15*

Stand therefore, having your loins girt about with truth, and having on the breastplate of righteousness;
Ephesians 6:14

Finally, brethren, whatsoever things are true, whatsoever things are honest, whatsoever things are just, whatsoever things are pure, whatsoever things are lovely, whatsoever things are of good report; if there be any virtue, and if there be any praise, think on these things. *Philippians 4:8*

Study to shew thyself approved unto God, a workman that needeth not to be ashamed, rightly dividing the word of truth. *2 Timothy 2:15*

And we know that the Son of God is come, and hath given us an understanding, that we may know Him that is true, and we are in Him that is true, even in His Son Jesus Christ. This is the true God, and eternal life.
1 John 5:20

THE SHEPHERD AND THE SHEEP

28

WHEN YOUR CHURCH DOES NOT SEEM TO BE GROWING SPIRITUALLY

━━◄►○◄►━━

And the Lord answered me, and said, Write the vision, and make it plain upon tables, that he may run that readeth it.   *Habakkuk 2:2*

For the priest's lips should keep knowledge, and they should seek the law at his mouth: for he is the messenger of the Lord of hosts.
                                Malachi 2:7

Go ye therefore, and teach all nations, baptizing them in the name of the Father, and of the Son, and of the Holy Ghost:

Teaching them to observe all things whatsoever I have commanded you: and, lo, I am with you alway, even unto the end of the world. Amen.

Matthew 28:19,20

But I have prayed for thee, that thy faith fail not: and when thou art converted, strengthen thy brethren.

Luke 22:32

Say not ye, There are yet four months, and then cometh harvest? behold, I say unto you, Lift up your eyes, and look on the fields; for they are white already to harvest.

And he that reapeth receiveth wages, and gathereth fruit unto life eternal: that both he that soweth and he that reapeth may rejoice together.

And herein is that saying true, One soweth, and another reapeth.

John 4:35-37

So when they had dined, Jesus

saith to Simon Peter, Simon, son of Jonas, lovest thou Me more than these? He saith unto Him, Yea, Lord; Thou knowest that I love Thee. He saith unto him, Feed My lambs.

He saith to him again the second time, Simon, son of Jonas, lovest thou Me? He saith unto Him, Yea, Lord; Thou knowest that I love Thee. He saith unto him, Feed My sheep.   *John 21:15,16*

For the perfecting of the saints, for the work of the ministry, for the edifying of the body of Christ:

Ephesians 4:12

Neglect not the gift that is in thee, which was given thee by prophecy, with the laying on of the hands of the presbytery.

Meditate upon these things; give thyself wholly to them; that thy profiting may appear to all.

Take heed unto thyself, and unto the doctrine; continue in them: for in doing this thou shalt both save thyself, and them that hear thee.

1 Timothy 4:14-16

Anything Permitted
Increases.

-MIKE MURDOCK

29

WHEN YOUR CHURCH MEMBERS BECOME CONTENTIOUS

Cast out the scorner, and contention shall go out; yea, strife and reproach shall cease.   *Proverbs 22:10*

Then there arose a reasoning among them, which of them should be greatest.

And Jesus, perceiving the thought of their heart, took a child, and set him by Him,

And said unto them, Whosoever shall receive this child in My name receiveth Me; and whosoever shall receive Me receiveth Him that sent Me: for he that is least among you all, the same shall be great.   *Luke 9:46-48*

For it hath been declared unto me
of you, my brethren, by them which are
of the house of Chloe, that there are
contentions among you.

Now this I say, that every one of
you saith, I am of Paul; and I of Apollos;
and I of Cephas; and I of Christ.

Is Christ divided? was Paul
crucified for you? or were ye baptized in
the name of Paul?

1 Corinthians 1:11-13

For ye are yet carnal: for whereas
there is among you envying, and strife,
and divisions, are ye not carnal, and
walk as men?

For while one saith, I am of Paul;
and another, I am of Apollos; are ye not
carnal?   *1 Corinthians 3:3,4*

How is it then, brethren? when ye
come together, every one of you hath a
psalm, hath a doctrine, hath a tongue,
hath a revelation, hath an interpretation. Let all things be done unto
edifying.

For God is not the author of
confusion, but of peace, as in all

churches of the saints.

1 Corinthians 14:26,33

For though we walk in the flesh, we do not war after the flesh:

For the weapons of our warfare are not carnal, but mighty through God to the pulling down of strong holds;

Casting down imaginations, and every high thing that exalteth itself against the knowledge of God, and bringing into captivity every thought to the obedience of Christ;

2 Corinthians 10:3-5

For I fear, lest, when I come, I shall not find you such as I would, and that I shall be found unto you such as ye would not: lest there be debates, envyings, wraths, strifes, backbitings, whisperings, swellings, tumults:

And lest, when I come again, my God will humble me among you, and that I shall bewail many which have sinned already, and have not repented of the uncleanness and fornication and lasciviousness which they have committed. *2 Corinthians 12:20,21*

And the servant of the Lord must not strive; but be gentle unto all men, apt to teach, patient,

In meekness instructing those that oppose themselves; if God peradventure will give them repentance to the acknowledging of the truth;

2 Timothy 2:24,25

For where envying and strife is, there is confusion and every evil work.

But the wisdom that is from above is first pure, then peaceable, gentle, and easy to be intreated, full of mercy and good fruits, without partiality, and without hypocrisy.   *James 3:16,17*

❦ 30 ❦

WHEN A CHURCH MEMBER BECOMES DISRESPECTFUL

Stand in awe, and sin not: commune with your own heart upon your bed, and be still.   *Psalm 4:4*

God is our refuge and strength, a very present help in trouble.

Psalm 46:1

The wicked is snared by the transgression of his lips: but the just shall come out of trouble.   *Proverbs 12:13*

Answer not a fool according to his folly, lest thou also be like unto him.

As coals are to burning coals, and wood to fire; so is a contentious man to kindle strife.   *Proverbs 26:4,21*

Behold, all they that were incensed against thee shall be ashamed and confounded: they shall be as nothing; and they that strive with thee shall perish. *Isaiah 41:11*

Blessed are ye, when men shall revile you, and persecute you, and shall say all manner of evil against you falsely, for My sake. *Matthew 5:11*

And if a kingdom be divided against itself, that kingdom cannot stand.

And if a house be divided against itself, that house cannot stand.

Mark 3:24,25

Dearly beloved, avenge not yourselves, but rather give place unto wrath: for it is written, Vengeance is mine; I will repay, saith the Lord.

Therefore if thine enemy hunger, feed him; if he thirst, give him drink: for in so doing thou shalt heap coals of fire on his head. *Romans 12:19,20*

See that none render evil for evil unto any man; but ever follow that which is good, both among yourselves, and to all men.   *1 Thessalonians 5:15*

But if ye have bitter envying and strife in your hearts, glory not, and lie not against the truth.   *James 3:14*

Not rendering evil for evil, or railing for railing: but contrariwise blessing; knowing that ye are thereunto called, that ye should inherit a blessing.
1 Peter 3:9

❧ 31 ❧

WHEN CHURCH MEMBERS CRITICIZE YOU UNFAIRLY

But Thou, O Lord, art a shield for me; my glory, and the lifter up of mine head. *Psalm 3:3*

For Thou wilt light my candle: the Lord my God will enlighten my darkness.

He delivereth me from mine enemies: yea, Thou liftest me up above those that rise up against me: Thou hast delivered me from the violent man. *Psalm 18:28,48*

The Lord is my light and my salvation; whom shall I fear? the Lord is the strength of my life; of whom shall I be afraid?

Wait on the Lord: be of good courage, and He shall strengthen thine heart: wait, I say, on the Lord.

Psalm 27:1,14

Why art thou cast down, O my soul? and why art thou disquieted within me? hope thou in God: for I shall yet praise Him, Who is the health of my countenance, and my God. *Psalm 42:11*

The ear that heareth the reproof of life abideth among the wise.

He that refuseth instruction despiseth his own soul: but he that heareth reproof getteth understanding.

Proverbs 15:31,32

And as ye would that men should do to you, do ye also to them likewise.

Luke 6:31

Let your speech be alway with grace, seasoned with salt, that ye may know how ye ought to answer every man. *Colossians 4:6*

Attack Is The Proof
Satan Anticipates
Your Success.

-MIKE MURDOCK

❧ 32 ❧

WHEN A CHURCH MEMBER SOWS DISHARMONY

These six things doth the Lord hate: yea, seven are an abomination unto Him:

A proud look, a lying tongue, and hands that shed innocent blood,

An heart that deviseth wicked imaginations, feet that be swift in running to mischief,

A false witness that speaketh lies, and he that soweth discord among brethren. *Proverbs 6:16-19*

Hatred stirreth up strifes: but love covereth all sins. *Proverbs 10:12*

Only by pride cometh contention:

but with the well advised is wisdom.
Proverbs 13:10

Cast out the scorner, and contention shall go out; yea, strife and reproach shall cease. *Proverbs 22:10*

As coals are to burning coals, and wood to fire; so is a contentious man to kindle strife. *Proverbs 26:21*

Why dost thou shew me iniquity, and cause me to behold grievance? for spoiling and violence are before me: and there are that raise up strife and contention.

Therefore the law is slacked, and judgment doth never go forth: for the wicked doth compass about the righteous; therefore wrong judgment proceedeth. *Habakkuk 1:3,4*

Put on therefore, as the elect of God, holy and beloved, bowels of mercies, kindness, humbleness of mind, meekness, longsuffering;
Colossians 3:12

Never Complain
About What
You Permit.

-MIKE MURDOCK

❧ 33 ❧

WHEN A CHURCH MEMBER LEAVES

He will keep the feet of His saints, and the wicked shall be silent in darkness; for by strength shall no man prevail.   *1 Samuel 2:9*

Yet through the scent of water it will bud, and bring forth boughs like a plant.

For there is hope of a tree, if it be cut down, that it will sprout again, and that the tender branch thereof will not cease.

Though the root thereof wax old in the earth, and the stock thereof die in the ground;   *Job 14:7-9*

I will be glad and rejoice in Thy mercy: for Thou hast considered my trouble; Thou hast known my soul in adversities;   *Psalm 31:7*

When thou liest down, thou shalt not be afraid: yea, thou shalt lie down, and thy sleep shall be sweet.
                    Proverbs 3:24

The Lord will not suffer the soul of the righteous to famish: but He casteth away the substance of the wicked.
The blessing of the Lord, it maketh rich, and He addeth no sorrow with it.
                    Proverbs 10:3,22

If thou faint in the day of adversity, thy strength is small.
                    Proverbs 24:10

Then came Peter to Him, and said, Lord, how oft shall my brother sin against me, and I forgive him? till seven times?   *Matthew 18:21*

Be ye therefore merciful, as your Father also is merciful.
Judge not, and ye shall not be

judged: condemn not, and ye shall not be condemned: forgive, and ye shall be forgiven: *Luke 6:36,37*

And be renewed in the spirit of your mind; *Ephesians 4:23*

Finally, my brethren, be strong in the Lord, and in the power of His might. *Ephesians 6:10*

Not that I speak in respect of want: for I have learned, in whatsoever state I am, therewith to be content.

I know both how to be abased, and I know how to abound: every where and in all things I am instructed both to be full and to be hungry, both to abound and to suffer need.

I can do all things through Christ which strengtheneth me.

Philippians 4:11-13

Preach the word; be instant in season, out of season; reprove, rebuke, exhort with all longsuffering and doctrine. *2 Timothy 4:2*

∼ 34 ∼

WHEN A CHURCH MEMBER SPREADS SLANDEROUS RUMORS

Thou shalt not go up and down as a talebearer among thy people: neither shalt thou stand against the blood of thy neighbour: I am the Lord.

Leviticus 19:16

For I have heard the slander of many: fear was on every side: while they took counsel together against me, they devised to take away my life.

But I trusted in Thee, O Lord: I said, Thou art my God. *Psalm 31:13,14*

All that hate me whisper together against me: against me do they devise my hurt. *Psalm 41:7*

He that hideth hatred with lying lips, and he that uttereth a slander, is a fool.   *Proverbs 10:18*

A talebearer revealeth secrets: but he that is of a faithful spirit concealeth the matter.   *Proverbs 11:13*

Poverty and shame shall be to him that refuseth instruction: but he that regardeth reproof shall be honoured.
                    Proverbs 13:18

A froward man soweth strife: and a whisperer separateth chief friends.
                    Proverbs 16:28

The words of a talebearer are as wounds, and they go down into the innermost parts of the belly.
                    Proverbs 18:8

He that goeth about as a talebearer revealeth secrets: therefore meddle not with him that flattereth with his lips.   *Proverbs 20:19*

Where no wood is, there the fire

goeth out: so where there is no talebearer, the strife ceaseth.

Proverbs 26:20

Then shalt thou call, and the Lord shall answer; thou shalt cry, and He shall say, Here I am. If thou take away from the midst of thee the yoke, the putting forth of the finger, and speaking vanity;   *Isaiah 58:9*

But speaking the truth in love, may grow up into Him in all things, which is the head, even Christ:

Ephesians 4:15

Preach the word; be instant in season, out of season; reprove, rebuke, exhort with all longsuffering and doctrine.   *2 Timothy 4:2*

Speak not evil one of another, brethren. He that speaketh evil of his brother, and judgeth his brother, speaketh evil of the law, and judgeth the law: but if thou judge the law, thou art not a doer of the law, but a judge.

James 4:11

False Accusation
Is The Last Stage
Before Supernatural
Promotion.

-MIKE MURDOCK

❧ 35 ❧

WHEN A CHURCH MEMBER MISINTERPRETS YOUR WORDS OR ACTIONS

After these things the word of the Lord came unto Abram in a vision, saying, Fear not, Abram: I am thy shield, and thy exceedingly great reward. *Genesis 15:1*

Happy art thou, O Israel: who is like unto thee, O people saved by the Lord, the shield of thy help, and Who is the sword of thy excellency! and thine enemies shall be found liars unto thee; and thou shalt tread upon their high places. *Deuteronomy 33:29*

The God of my rock; in Him will I trust: He is my shield, and the horn of my salvation, my high tower, and my refuge, my saviour; Thou savest me from violence.

I will call on the Lord, Who is worthy to be praised: so shall I be saved from mine enemies.

2 Samuel 22:3,4

Lord, how are they increased that trouble me! many are they that rise up against me.

Many there be which say of my soul, There is no help for him in God.

But thou, O Lord, art a shield for me; my glory, and the lifter up of mine head. *Psalm 3:1-3*

Thou hast also given me the shield of Thy salvation: and Thy right hand hath holden me up, and Thy gentleness hath made me great. *Psalm 18:35*

Thou preparest a table before me in the presence of mine enemies: Thou anointest my head with oil; my cup runneth over. *Psalm 23:5*

What time I am afraid, I will trust in Thee.

In God I will praise His word, in God I have put my trust; I will not fear what flesh can do unto me.

In God have I put my trust: I will not be afraid what man can do unto me.
Psalm 56:3,4,11

For the Lord God is a sun and shield: the Lord will give grace and glory: no good thing will He withhold from them that walk uprightly.
Psalm 84:11

He shall cover thee with His feathers, and under His wings shalt thou trust: His truth shall be thy shield and buckler. *Psalm 91:4*

Thou art my hiding place and my shield: I hope in Thy word.
Psalm 119:114

When thou liest down, thou shalt not be afraid: yea, thou shalt lie down, and thy sleep shall be sweet.
Proverbs 3:24

What You Cannot
　　Give Another
Is The Gift
　　That Drives Them
Toward God.

-MIKE MURDOCK

❧ 36 ❧

WHEN A CHURCH MEMBER HAS UNREALISTIC EXPECTATIONS OF YOU

My lips shall not speak wickedness, nor my tongue utter deceit.
Job 27:4

Cease from anger, and forsake wrath: fret not thyself in any wise to do evil.
Psalm 37:8

In my distress I cried unto the Lord, and He heard me.
Deliver my soul, O Lord, from lying lips, and from a deceitful tongue.
Psalm 120:1,2

Set a watch, O Lord, before my mouth; keep the door of my lips.

Psalm 141:3

He that keepeth his mouth keepeth his life: but he that openeth wide his lips shall have destruction.

Proverbs 13:3

He that is slow to wrath is of great understanding: but he that is hasty of spirit exalteth folly.   *Proverbs 14:29*

A soft answer turneth away wrath: but grievous words stir up anger.

Proverbs 15:1

Seest thou a man that is hasty in his words? there is more hope of a fool than of him.   *Proverbs 29:20*

Be not hasty in thy spirit to be angry: for anger resteth in the bosom of fools.   *Ecclesiastes 7:9*

But I say unto you, That every idle word that men shall speak, they shall

give account thereof in the day of
judgment.

For by thy words thou shalt be
justified, and by thy words thou shalt
be condemned.   *Matthew 12:36,37*

Be ye angry, and sin not: let not
the sun go down upon your wrath:
Ephesians 4:26

Wherefore, my beloved brethren,
let every man be swift to hear, slow to
speak, slow to wrath:

For the wrath of man worketh not
the righteousness of God.

Wherefore lay apart all filthiness
and superfluity of naughtiness, and
receive with meekness the engrafted
word, which is able to save your souls.
James 1:19-21

You Are Not Responsible
For The Pain
Of Those Who Ignore
Your Counsel.

-MIKE MURDOCK

❧ 37 ❧

WHEN A CHURCH MEMBER IGNORES YOUR COUNSEL

I will bless the Lord, Who hath given me counsel: my reins also instruct me in the night seasons.

I have set the Lord always before me: because He is at my right hand, I shall not be moved.   *Psalm 16:7,8*

Judge me, O Lord; for I have walked in mine integrity: I have trusted also in the Lord; therefore I shall not slide.

Examine me, O Lord, and prove me; try my reins and my heart.
                                    Psalm 26:1,2

And the peace of God, which passeth all understanding, shall keep your hearts and minds through Christ Jesus.

Finally, brethren, whatsoever things are true, whatsoever things are honest, whatsoever things are just, whatsoever things are pure, whatsoever things are lovely, whatsoever things are of good report; if there be any virtue, and if there be any praise, think on these things.   *Philippians 4:7,8*

For God hath not given us the spirit of fear; but of power, and of love, and of a sound mind.   *2 Timothy 1:7*

❧ 38 ❧

WHEN A CHURCH MEMBER DEMANDS UNEARNED AUTHORITY

I will instruct thee and teach thee in the way which thou shalt go: I will guide thee with Mine eye.   *Psalm 32:8*

Be not afraid of sudden fear, neither of the desolation of the wicked, when it cometh.
For the Lord shall be thy confidence, and shall keep thy foot from being taken.   *Proverbs 3:25,26*

Poverty and shame shall be to him that refuseth instruction: but he that regardeth reproof shall be honoured.
Proverbs 13:18

Moreover if thy brother shall trespass against thee, go and tell him his fault between thee and him alone: if he shall hear thee, thou hast gained thy brother.   *Matthew 18:15*

Take heed to yourselves: If thy brother trespass against thee, rebuke him; and if he repent, forgive him.
Luke 17:3

Now we exhort you, brethren, warn them that are unruly, comfort the feebleminded, support the weak, be patient toward all men.
1 Thessalonians 5:14

Them that sin rebuke before all, that others also may fear.
1 Timothy 5:20

If any of you lack wisdom, let him ask of God, that giveth to all men liberally, and upbraideth not; and it shall be given him.   *James 1:5*

Those Unwilling
To Wait
Are Unqualified
To Rule.

-MIKE MURDOCK

❦ 39 ❦

WHEN A CHURCH MEMBER OFFERS DECEPTIVE FLATTERY

Let me not, I pray you, accept any man's person, neither let me give flattering titles unto man.

For I know not to give flattering titles; in so doing my maker would soon take me away.   *Job 32:21,22*

They speak vanity every one with his neighbour: with flattering lips and with a double heart do they speak.

Psalm 12:2

The words of his mouth were smoother than butter, but war was in his heart: his words were softer than

oil, yet were they drawn swords.
Psalm 55:21

Discretion shall preserve thee, understanding shall keep thee:
Proverbs 2:11

A man that flattereth his neighbour spreadeth a net for his feet.
Proverbs 29:5

Woe unto you, when all men shall speak well of you! for so did their fathers to the false prophets. *Luke 6:26*

For neither at any time used we flattering words, as ye know, nor a cloak of covetousness; God is witness:
1 Thessalonians 2:5

Those Who Disagree
With Your Goals
Will Disagree
With Your Decisions.

-MIKE MURDOCK

YOUR DEACONS, ELDERS, STAFF AND VOLUNTEER MINISTRY ASSOCIATES

∞ 40 ∞

WHEN AN ASSOCIATE DISAGREES WITH YOUR DOCTRINE

Lord, who shall abide in Thy tabernacle? who shall dwell in Thy holy hill?

He that walketh uprightly, and worketh righteousness, and speaketh the truth in his heart.

He that backbiteth not with his tongue, nor doeth evil to his neighbour, nor taketh up a reproach against his neighbour.   *Psalm 15:1-3*

That they may shoot in secret at the perfect: suddenly do they shoot at him, and fear not.

But God shall shoot at them with an arrow; suddenly shall they be wounded.   *Psalm 64:4,7*

Princes also did sit and speak against me: but Thy servant did meditate in Thy statutes. *Psalm 119:23*

Set a watch, O Lord, before my mouth; keep the door of my lips.
                    Psalm 141:3

The lips of the righteous know what is acceptable: but the mouth of the wicked speaketh frowardness.
                    Proverbs 10:32

The lip of truth shall be established for ever: but a lying tongue is but for a moment.   *Proverbs 12:19*

He that keepeth his mouth keepeth his life: but he that openeth wide his lips shall have destruction.
Proverbs 13:3

A soft answer turneth away wrath: but grievous words stir up anger.
Proverbs 15:1

And be renewed in the spirit of your mind;

Let no corrupt communication proceed out of your mouth, but that which is good to the use of edifying, that it may minister grace unto the hearers.

Let all bitterness, and wrath, and anger, and clamour, and evil speaking, be put away from you, with all malice:
Ephesians 4:23,29,31

For he that will love life, and see good days, let him refrain his tongue from evil, and his lips that they speak no guile: *1 Peter 3:10*

❧ 41 ❧

WHEN AN ASSOCIATE DOES NOT SHARE YOUR VISION

For I have heard the slander of many: fear was on every side: while they took counsel together against me, they devised to take away my life.

Make Thy face to shine upon Thy servant: save me for Thy mercies' sake.

Psalm 31:13,16

For the Lord God will help me; therefore shall I not be confounded: therefore have I set my face like a flint, and I know that I shall not be ashamed.

Isaiah 50:7

But I will deliver thee in that day, saith the Lord: and thou shalt not be given into the hand of the men of whom thou art afraid.

For I will surely deliver thee, and thou shalt not fall by the sword, but thy life shall be for a prey unto thee: because thou hast put thy trust in Me, saith the Lord. *Jeremiah 39:17,18*

Can two walk together, except they be agreed? *Amos 3:3*

Let all bitterness, and wrath, and anger, and clamour, and evil speaking, be put away from you, with all malice: *Ephesians 4:31*

Every Step
Toward Order
Exposes Those Who
Do Not Belong.

-MIKE MURDOCK

≈ 42 ≈

WHEN AN ASSOCIATE CHALLENGES YOUR LEADERSHIP

And Abram said unto Lot, Let there be no strife, I pray thee, between me and thee, and between my herdmen and thy herdmen; for we be brethren.

Genesis 13:8

Now therefore go, and I will be with thy mouth, and teach thee what thou shalt say.   *Exodus 4:12*

Let the words of my mouth, and the meditation of my heart, be acceptable in Thy sight, O Lord, my strength, and my redeemer.

Psalm 19:14

Cease from anger, and forsake wrath: fret not thyself in any wise to do evil.   *Psalm 37:8*

And hide not Thy face from Thy servant; for I am in trouble: hear me speedily.
Draw nigh unto my soul, and redeem it: deliver me because of mine enemies.   *Psalm 69:17,18*

Help me, O Lord my God: O save me according to Thy mercy:
That they may know that this is Thy hand; that Thou, Lord, hast done it.
Let them curse, but bless Thou: when they arise, let them be ashamed; but let Thy servant rejoice.
Psalm 109:26-28

Answer not a fool according to his folly, lest thou also be like unto him.
Answer a fool according to his folly, lest he be wise in his own conceit.
Proverbs 26:4,5

Behold, all they that were incensed against thee shall be ashamed and

confounded: they shall be as nothing;
and they that strive with thee shall
perish.   *Isaiah 41:11*

For I will give you a mouth and
wisdom, which all your adversaries
shall not be able to gainsay nor resist.
                           Luke 21:15

For the weapons of our warfare are
not carnal, but mighty through God to
the pulling down of strong holds;
Casting down imaginations, and
every high thing that exalteth itself
against the knowledge of God, and
bringing into captivity every thought to
the obedience of Christ;
                    2 Corinthians 10:4,5

Let all bitterness, and wrath, and
anger, and clamour, and evil speaking,
be put away from you, with all malice:
                        Ephesians 4:31

Let your speech be alway with
grace, seasoned with salt, that ye may
know how ye ought to answer every
man.   *Colossians 4:6*

❧ 43 ❧

WHEN AN ASSOCIATE DISREGARDS YOUR ADVICE

Go not forth hastily to strive, lest thou know not what to do in the end thereof, when thy neighbour hath put thee to shame.   *Proverbs 25:8*

Behold My servant, whom I have chosen; My beloved, in whom My soul is well pleased: I will put My Spirit upon him, and he shall shew judgment to the Gentiles.

He shall not strive, nor cry; neither shall any man hear his voice in the streets.

A bruised reed shall he not break, and smoking flax shall he not quench,

till he send forth judgment unto victory.
Matthew 12:18-20

Moreover if thy brother shall trespass against thee, go and tell him his fault between thee and him alone: if he shall hear thee, thou hast gained thy brother.

But if he will not hear thee, then take with thee one or two more, that in the mouth of two or three witnesses every word may be established.

And if he shall neglect to hear them, tell it unto the church: but if he neglect to hear the church, let him be unto thee as an heathen man and a publican.   *Matthew 18:15-17*

Let no man despise thy youth; but be thou an example of the believers, in word, in conversation, in charity, in spirit, in faith, in purity.

1 Timothy 4:12

Rebuke not an elder, but intreat him as a father; and the younger men as brethren;   *1 Timothy 5:1*

Of these things put them in
remembrance, charging them before the
Lord that they strive not about words to
no profit, but to the subverting of the
hearers.

And the servant of the Lord must
not strive; but be gentle unto all men,
apt to teach, patient, *2 Timothy 2:14,24*

In all things shewing thyself a
pattern of good works: in doctrine
shewing   uncorruptness,   gravity,
sincerity,   *Titus 2:7*

Remember them which have the
rule over you, who have spoken unto
you the word of God: whose faith follow,
considering the end of their conversation.   *Hebrews 13:7*

But the wisdom that is from above
is first pure, then peaceable, gentle, and
easy to be intreated, full of mercy and
good fruits, without partiality, and
without hypocrisy.   *James 3:17*

❧ 44 ❧

WHEN AN ASSOCIATE HAS MADE A SERIOUS MISTAKE

He that covereth a transgression seeketh love; but he that repeateth a matter separateth very friends.

A friend loveth at all times, and a brother is born for adversity.

Proverbs 17:9,17

For a just man falleth seven times, and riseth up again: but the wicked shall fall into mischief.   *Proverbs 24:16*

Confidence in an unfaithful man in time of trouble is like a broken tooth, and a foot out of joint.   *Proverbs 25:19*

Blessed are the merciful: for they

shall obtain mercy. *Matthew 5:7*

Brethren, if a man be overtaken in a fault, ye which are spiritual, restore such an one in the spirit of meekness; considering thyself, lest thou also be tempted. *Galatians 6:1*

And above all these things put on charity, which is the bond of perfectness. *Colossians 3:14*

But thou, O man of God, flee these things; and follow after righteousness, godliness, faith, love, patience, meekness. *1 Timothy 6:11*

And let us consider one another to provoke unto love and to good works:
Hebrews 10:24

Not rendering evil for evil, or railing for railing: but contrariwise blessing; knowing that ye are thereunto called, that ye should inherit a blessing.
1 Peter 3:9

～ 45 ～

WHEN AN ASSOCIATE
BETRAYS A CONFIDENCE

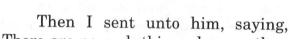

Then I sent unto him, saying, There are no such things done as thou sayest, but thou feignest them out of thine own heart.

For they all made us afraid, saying, Their hands shall be weakened from the work, that it be not done. Now therefore, O God, strengthen my hands.
Nehemiah 6:8,9

Stand in awe, and sin not: commune with your own heart upon your bed, and be still. *Psalm 4:4*

But as for me, I will come into Thy house in the multitude of Thy mercy: and in Thy fear will I worship toward Thy holy temple. *Psalm 5:7*

Trust in the Lord with all thine heart; and lean not unto thine own understanding.

In all thy ways acknowledge Him, and He shall direct thy paths.

Proverbs 3:5,6

He that handleth a matter wisely shall find good: and whoso trusteth in the Lord, happy is he.   *Proverbs 16:20*

Debate thy cause with thy neighbour himself; and discover not a secret to another: *Proverbs 25:9*

Confidence in an unfaithful man in time of trouble is like a broken tooth, and a foot out of joint.   *Proverbs 25:19*

He that is of a proud heart stirreth up strife: but he that putteth his trust in the Lord shall be made fat.

Proverbs 28:25

The fear of man bringeth a snare: but whoso putteth his trust in the Lord shall be safe.   *Proverbs 29:25*

Thou wilt keep him in perfect peace, whose mind is stayed on Thee: because he trusteth in Thee.

Isaiah 26:3

Be ye angry, and sin not: let not the sun go down upon your wrath:

And grieve not the Holy Spirit of God, whereby ye are sealed unto the day of redemption.

Let all bitterness, and wrath, and anger, and clamour, and evil speaking, be put away from you, with all malice:

Ephesians 4:26,30,31

Looking diligently lest any man fail of the grace of God; lest any root of bitterness springing up trouble you, and thereby many be defiled;

Hebrews 12:15

≈ 46 ≈

WHEN AN ASSOCIATE TALKS TO OTHERS ABOUT YOUR FAULTS

Mine enemies speak evil of me, When shall he die, and his name perish?

And if he come to see me, he speaketh vanity: his heart gathereth iniquity to itself; when he goeth abroad, he telleth it.

All that hate me whisper together against me: against me do they devise my hurt.

But Thou, O Lord, be merciful unto me, and raise me up, that I may requite them.

By this I know that Thou favourest me, because mine enemy doth not triumph over me.   *Psalm 41:5-7,10,11*

My heart is fixed, O God, my heart is fixed: I will sing and give praise.

Psalm 57:7

For the sin of their mouth and the words of their lips let them even be taken in their pride: and for cursing and lying which they speak.

Psalm 59:12

Hide me from the secret counsel of the wicked; from the insurrection of the workers of iniquity:

Who whet their tongue like a sword, and bend their bows to shoot their arrows, even bitter words:

Psalm 64:2,3

And ye shall be hated of all men for My name's sake: but he that endureth to the end shall be saved.

Matthew 10:22

Blessed are ye, when men shall hate you, and when they shall separate you from their company, and shall reproach you, and cast out your name

as evil, for the Son of man's sake.
Luke 6:22

Be not overcome of evil, but overcome evil with good. *Romans 12:21*

And labour, working with our own hands: being reviled, we bless; being persecuted, we suffer it:
1 Corinthians 4:12

And the Lord shall deliver me from every evil work, and will preserve me unto His heavenly kingdom: to Whom be glory for ever and ever. Amen.
2 Timothy 4:18

Wherefore, my beloved brethren, let every man be swift to hear, slow to speak, slow to wrath: *James 1:19*

Who, when He was reviled, reviled not again; when He suffered, He threatened not; but committed Himself to Him that judgeth righteously:
1 Peter 2:23

Not rendering evil for evil, or railing for railing: but contrariwise blessing; knowing that ye are thereunto called, that ye should inherit a blessing.

For he that will love life, and see good days, let him refrain his tongue from evil, and his lips that they speak no guile:

Having a good conscience; that, whereas they speak evil of you, as of evildoers, they may be ashamed that falsely accuse your good conversation in Christ.

For it is better, if the will of God be so, that ye suffer for well doing, than for evil doing.   *1 Peter 3:9,10,16,17*

Wherein they think it strange that ye run not with them to the same excess of riot, speaking evil of you:

If ye be reproached for the name of Christ, happy are ye; for the spirit of glory and of God resteth upon you: on their part He is evil spoken of, but on your part He is glorified.   *1 Peter 4:4,14*

Nothing Is Ever
As It First Appears.

-MIKE MURDOCK

⚜ 47 ⚜

WHEN YOU HAVE OFFENDED AN ASSOCIATE

Surely it is meet to be said unto God, I have borne chastisement, I will not offend any more:

That which I see not teach Thou me: if I have done iniquity, I will do no more.   *Job 34:31,32*

A brother offended is harder to be won than a strong city: and their contentions are like the bars of a castle.
Proverbs 18:19

If the spirit of the ruler rise up against thee, leave not thy place; for yielding pacifieth great offences.
Ecclesiastes 10:4

Then came His disciples, and said

unto Him, Knowest Thou that the Pharisees were offended, after they heard this saying?

But He answered and said, Every plant, which My heavenly Father hath not planted, shall be rooted up.

Let them alone: they be blind leaders of the blind. And if the blind lead the blind, both shall fall into the ditch.   *Matthew 15:12-14*

Woe unto the world because of offences! for it must needs be that offences come; but woe to that man by whom the offence cometh!

Matthew 18:7

And when ye stand praying, forgive, if ye have ought against any: that your Father also which is in heaven may forgive you your trespasses.   *Mark 11:25*

And forgive us our sins; for we also forgive every one that is indebted to us. And lead us not into temptation; but deliver us from evil.   *Luke 11:4*

Then said He unto the disciples, It is impossible but that offences will come: but woe unto him, through whom they come!

Take heed to yourselves: If thy brother trespass against thee, rebuke him; and if he repent, forgive him.

And if he trespass against thee seven times in a day, and seven times in a day turn again to thee, saying, I repent; thou shalt forgive him.

Luke 17:1,3,4

And herein do I exercise myself, to have always a conscience void of offence toward God, and toward men. *Acts 24:16*

It is good neither to eat flesh, nor to drink wine, nor any thing whereby thy brother stumbleth, or is offended, or is made weak. *Romans 14:21*

Now I beseech you, brethren, mark them which cause divisions and offences contrary to the doctrine which ye have learned; and avoid them.

Romans 16:17

Wherefore, if meat make my brother to offend, I will eat no flesh while the world standeth, lest I make my brother to offend.

1 Corinthians 8:13

Give none offence, neither to the Jews, nor to the Gentiles, nor to the church of God: *1 Corinthians 10:32*

Giving no offence in any thing, that the ministry be not blamed:

2 Corinthians 6:3

And be ye kind one to another, tenderhearted, forgiving one another, even as God for Christ's sake hath forgiven you. *Ephesians 4:32*

Forbearing one another, and forgiving one another, if any man have a quarrel against any: even as Christ forgave you, so also do ye.

Colossians 3:13

For in many things we offend all. If any man offend not in word, the same

is a perfect man, and able also to bridle
the whole body.   *James 3:2*

Confess your faults one to another,
and pray one for another, that ye may
be healed. The effectual fervent prayer
of a righteous man availeth much.
                                   James 5:16

If we confess our sins, He is
faithful and just to forgive us our sins,
and to cleanse us from all unrighteous-
ness.   *1 John 1:9*

Your Success Is
Determined By
What You Are Willing
To Ignore.

-MIKE MURDOCK

48

WHEN YOU ARE UNJUSTLY ACCUSED BY AN ASSOCIATE

Keep me as the apple of the eye, hide me under the shadow of Thy wings,

From the wicked that oppress me, from my deadly enemies, who compass me about.   *Psalm 17:8,9*

For in the time of trouble He shall hide me in His pavilion: in the secret of His tabernacle shall He hide me; He shall set me up upon a rock.

Psalm 27:5

Thou shalt hide them in the secret of Thy presence from the pride of man: Thou shalt keep them secretly in a

pavilion from the strife of tongues.
Psalm 31:20

Thou art my hiding place; Thou shalt preserve me from trouble; Thou shalt compass me about with songs of deliverance. *Psalm 32:7*

My confusion is continually before me, and the shame of my face hath covered me,
For the voice of him that reproacheth and blasphemeth; by reason of the enemy and avenger.
All this is come upon us; yet have we not forgotten Thee, neither have we dealt falsely in Thy covenant.
Our heart is not turned back, neither have our steps declined from Thy way; *Psalm 44:15-18*

From the end of the earth will I cry unto Thee, when my heart is overwhelmed: lead me to the rock that is higher than I.
For Thou hast been a shelter for

me, and a strong tower from the enemy.
Psalm 61:2,3

Hide not Thy face from me in the
day when I am in trouble; incline Thine
ear unto me: in the day when I call
answer me speedily.   *Psalm 102:2*

Hear me speedily, O Lord: my
spirit faileth: hide not Thy face from
me, lest I be like unto them that go
down into the pit.
Cause me to hear Thy lovingkindness in the morning; for in Thee do I
trust: cause me to know the way
wherein I should walk; for I lift up my
soul unto Thee.
Deliver me, O Lord, from mine
enemies: I flee unto Thee to hide me.
Teach me to do Thy will; for Thou
art my God: Thy spirit is good; lead me
into the land of uprightness.
Quicken me, O Lord, for Thy
name's sake: for Thy righteousness'
sake bring my soul out of trouble.
Psalm 143:7-11

Come, My people, enter thou into thy chambers, and shut thy doors about thee: hide thyself as it were for a little moment, until the indignation be overpast. *Isaiah 26:20*

And a man shall be as an hiding place from the wind, and a covert from the tempest; as rivers of water in a dry place, as the shadow of a great rock in a weary land. *Isaiah 32:2*

Judge not, and ye shall not be judged: condemn not, and ye shall not be condemned: forgive, and ye shall be forgiven: *Luke 6:37*

And forgive us our sins; for we also forgive every one that is indebted to us. And lead us not into temptation; but deliver us from evil. *Luke 11:4*

Then said Jesus, Father, forgive them; for they know not what they do. And they parted His raiment, and cast lots. *Luke 23:34*

And labour, working with our own hands: being reviled, we bless; being persecuted, we suffer it:

1 Corinthians 4:12

And be ye kind one to another, tenderhearted, forgiving one another, even as God for Christ's sake hath forgiven you. *Ephesians 4:32*

For the which cause I also suffer these things: nevertheless I am not ashamed: for I know Whom I have believed, and am persuaded that He is able to keep that which I have committed unto Him against that day.

2 Timothy 1:12

Who, when He was reviled, reviled not again; when He suffered, He threatened not; but committed Himself to Him that judgeth righteously:

1 Peter 2:23

Those Without Your Memories
Cannot Feel Your Pain.
Those Who Cannot Feel Your Pain
May Misunderstand Your Goals.
Those Who Misunderstand Your Goals
May Despise Your Decisions.
Those Who Consistently Disagree
With Your Decisions Will
Eventually Become Your Adversary.

-MIKE MURDOCK

～ 49 ～

WHEN YOU FACE
CONSTANT RESISTANCE
BY AN ASSOCIATE

And the Spirit of God came upon Zechariah the son of Jehoiada the priest, which stood above the people, and said unto them, Thus saith God, Why transgress ye the commandments of the Lord, that ye cannot prosper? because ye have forsaken the Lord, He hath also forsaken you.

And they conspired against him, and stoned him with stones at the commandment of the king in the court of the house of the Lord.

2 Chronicles 24:20,21

And conspired all of them together to come and to fight against Jerusalem, and to hinder it.

Nevertheless we made our prayer unto our God, and set a watch against them day and night, because of them.

Nehemiah 4:8,9

O Lord my God, in Thee do I put my trust: save me from all them that persecute me, and deliver me:

Psalm 7:1

My times are in Thy hand: deliver me from the hand of mine enemies, and from them that persecute me.

Psalm 31:15

All Thy commandments are faithful: they persecute me wrongfully; help Thou me.

Many are my persecutors and mine enemies; yet do I not decline from Thy testimonies.

Princes have persecuted me without a cause: but my heart standeth in awe of Thy word.

Psalm 119:86,157,161

For the enemy hath persecuted my soul; he hath smitten my life down to the ground; he hath made me to dwell in darkness, as those that have been long dead.

Therefore is my spirit over-whelmed within me; my heart within me is desolate.

Cause me to hear Thy lovingkindness in the morning; for in Thee do I trust: cause me to know the way wherein I should walk; for I lift up my soul unto Thee.

Deliver me, O Lord, from mine enemies: I flee unto Thee to hide me.

Teach me to do Thy will; for Thou art my God: Thy spirit is good; lead me into the land of uprightness.

Psalm 143:3,4,8-10

O Lord, Thou knowest: remember me, and visit me, and revenge me of my persecutors; take me not away in Thy longsuffering: know that for Thy sake I have suffered rebuke.

Thy words were found, and I did

eat them; and Thy word was unto me the joy and rejoicing of mine heart: for I am called by Thy name, O Lord God of hosts.   *Jeremiah 15:15,16*

Then the king commanded, and they brought Daniel, and cast him into the den of lions. Now the king spake and said unto Daniel, Thy God Whom thou servest continually, He will deliver thee.   *Daniel 6:16*

Blessed are ye, when men shall revile you, and persecute you, and shall say all manner of evil against you falsely, for My sake.   *Matthew 5:11*

Then the Pharisees went out, and held a council against Him, how they might destroy Him.

And Jesus knew their thoughts, and said unto them, Every kingdom divided against itself is brought to desolation; and every city or house divided against itself shall not stand:

He that is not with Me is against Me; and he that gathereth not with Me scattereth abroad. *Matthew 12:14,25,30*

Because the carnal mind is enmity against God: for it is not subject to the law of God, neither indeed can be.

What shall we then say to these things? If God be for us, who can be against us?   *Romans 8:7,31*

Forbearing one another, and forgiving one another, if any man have a quarrel against any: even as Christ forgave you, so also do ye.

Colossians 3:13

For consider Him that endured such contradiction of sinners against Himself, lest ye be wearied and faint in your minds.

Ye have not yet resisted unto blood, striving against sin.

Hebrews 12:3,4

But if ye have bitter envying and strife in your hearts, glory not, and lie not against the truth.   *James 3:14*

Any Movement
Toward Order
Generates Pleasure.

-MIKE MURDOCK

YOUR DAILY SCHEDULE

～ 50 ～

WHEN YOU FEEL DISORGANIZED

━━━◆◦◦◦◆━━━

The Lord is my shepherd; I shall not want.   *Psalm 23:1*

Shew me Thy ways, O Lord; teach me Thy paths.   *Psalm 25:4*

O fear the Lord, ye His saints: for there is no want to them that fear Him.
Psalm 34:9

Behold, as the eyes of servants look unto the hand of their masters, and

as the eyes of a maiden unto the hand
of her mistress; so our eyes wait upon
the Lord our God, until that He have
mercy upon us.   *Psalm 123:2*

Go to the ant, thou sluggard;
consider her ways, and be wise:
Which having no guide, overseer,
or ruler,
Provideth her meat in the summer,
and gathereth her food in the harvest.
How long wilt thou sleep, O
sluggard? when wilt thou arise out of
thy sleep?
Yet a little sleep, a little slumber, a
little folding of the hands to sleep:
                    Proverbs 6:6-10

The hand of the diligent shall bear
rule: but the slothful shall be under
tribute.
The slothful man roasteth not that
which he took in hunting: but the
substance of a diligent man is precious.
                  Proverbs 12:24,27

The soul of the sluggard desireth,

and hath nothing: but the soul of the diligent shall be made fat.

Proverbs 13:4

The thoughts of the diligent tend only to plenteousness; but of every one that is hasty only to want.

Proverbs 21:5

Seest thou a man diligent in his business? he shall stand before kings; he shall not stand before mean men.

Proverbs 22:29

Be thou diligent to know the state of thy flocks, and look well to thy herds.

Proverbs 27:23

For God is not the author of confusion, but of peace, as in all churches of the saints.

1 Corinthians 14:33

And we have sent with them our brother, whom we have oftentimes proved diligent in many things, but now much more diligent, upon the great confidence which I have in you.

2 Corinthians 8:22

Tired Eyes Rarely See
A Good Future.

-MIKE MURDOCK

~ 51 ~

WHEN YOU OVER SCHEDULE YOURSELF

And Moses said unto them, Stand still, and I will hear what the Lord will command concerning you. *Numbers 9:8*

And as they were going down to the end of the city, Samuel said to Saul, Bid the servant pass on before us, and he passed on, but stand thou still a while, that I may shew thee the word of God. *1 Samuel 9:27*

And after the earthquake a fire; but the Lord was not in the fire: and after the fire a still small voice.

1 Kings 19:12

Ye shall not need to fight in this battle: set yourselves, stand ye still,

and see the salvation of the Lord with
you, O Judah and Jerusalem: fear not,
nor be dismayed; tomorrow go out
against them: for the Lord will be with
you.   *2 Chronicles 20:17*

Stand in awe, and sin not:
commune with your own heart upon
your bed, and be still.   *Psalm 4:4*

Be still, and know that I am God: I
will be exalted among the heathen, I
will be exalted in the earth.
                                   Psalm 46:10

From the end of the earth will I cry
unto Thee, when my heart is over-
whelmed: lead me to the rock that is
higher than I.   *Psalm 61:2*

A faithful man shall abound with
blessings: but he that maketh haste to
be rich shall not be innocent.
                                  Proverbs 28:20

Whoso keepeth the commandment
shall feel no evil thing: and a wise
man's heart discerneth both time and
judgment.   *Ecclesiastes 8:5*

And the work of righteousness shall be peace; and the effect of righteousness quietness and assurance for ever.

And My people shall dwell in a peaceable habitation, and in sure dwellings, and in quiet resting places;

Isaiah 32:17,18

But Martha was cumbered about much serving, and came to Him, and said, Lord, dost Thou not care that my sister hath left me to serve alone? bid her therefore that she help me.

And Jesus answered and said unto her, Martha, Martha, thou art careful and troubled about many things:

But one thing is needful: and Mary hath chosen that good part, which shall not be taken away from her.

Luke 10:40-42

Those Who Trivialize
Your Time Are
Unworthy Of It.

-MIKE MURDOCK

∾ 52 ∾

WHEN PEOPLE UNNECESSARILY CONSUME YOUR TIME

For in the time of trouble He shall hide me in His pavilion: in the secret of His tabernacle shall He hide me; He shall set me up upon a rock. *Psalm 27:5*

He that is slow to wrath is of great understanding: but he that is hasty of spirit exalteth folly.   *Proverbs 14:29*

A soft answer turneth away wrath: but grievous words stir up anger.

A wrathful man stirreth up strife: but he that is slow to anger appeaseth strife.   *Proverbs 15:1,18*

He that is slow to anger is better than the mighty; and he that ruleth his

spirit than he that taketh a city.
Proverbs 16:32

The discretion of a man deferreth
his anger; and it is his glory to pass over
a transgression.   *Proverbs 19:11*

It is an honour for a man to cease
from strife: but every fool will be
meddling.   *Proverbs 20:3*

By long forbearing is a prince
persuaded, and a soft tongue breaketh
the bone.   *Proverbs 25:15*

Better is the end of a thing than
the beginning thereof: and the patient
in spirit is better than the proud in
spirit.   *Ecclesiastes 7:8*

Come, My people, enter thou into
thy chambers, and shut thy doors about
thee: hide thyself as it were for a little
moment, until the indignation be
overpast.   *Isaiah 26:20*

Come unto Me, all ye that labour
and are heavy laden, and I will give you
rest.

Take My yoke upon you, and learn of Me; for I am meek and lowly in heart: and ye shall find rest unto your souls.
Matthew 11:28,29

And He said unto them, Come ye yourselves apart into a desert place, and rest a while: for there were many coming and going, and they had no leisure so much as to eat.

And they departed into a desert place by ship privately. *Mark 6:31,32*

And the servant of the Lord must not strive; but be gentle unto all men, apt to teach, patient, *2 Timothy 2:24*

To speak evil of no man, to be no brawlers, but gentle, shewing all meekness unto all men. *Titus 3:2*

There remaineth therefore a rest to the people of God.

For he that is entered into his rest, he also hath ceased from his own works, as God did from His.
Hebrews 4:9,10

Follow peace with all men, and holiness, without which no man shall see the Lord: *Hebrews 12:14*

But the wisdom that is from above is first pure, then peaceable, gentle, and easy to be intreated, full of mercy and good fruits, without partiality, and without hypocrisy.

And the fruit of righteousness is sown in peace of them that make peace.
James 3:17,18

Your Respect For Time Is
A Prediction Of Your
Financial Future.

-MIKE MURDOCK

∼ 53 ∼

WHEN YOU ARE
ESTABLISHING YOUR
GOALS

And the Lord said unto Moses,
Depart, and go up hence, thou and the
people which thou hast brought up out
of the land of Egypt, unto the land
which I sware unto Abraham, to Isaac,
and to Jacob, saying, Unto thy seed will
I give it:

And I will send an angel before
thee; and I will drive out the Canaanite,
the Amorite, and the Hittite, and the
Perizzite, the Hivite, and the Jebusite:

Exodus 33:1,2

And they commanded the people,
saying, When ye see the ark of the
covenant of the Lord your God, and the
priests the Levites bearing it, then ye

shall remove from your place, and go after it.

Yet there shall be a space between you and it, about two thousand cubits by measure: come not near unto it, that ye may know the way by which ye must go: for ye have not passed this way heretofore. *Joshua 3:3,4*

And they said unto him, Ask counsel, we pray thee, of God, that we may know whether our way which we go shall be prosperous.

And the priest said unto them, Go in peace: before the Lord is your way wherein ye go. *Judges 18:5,6*

And it came to pass, when I heard these words, that I sat down and wept, and mourned certain days, and fasted, and prayed before the God of heaven,

Let Thine ear now be attentive, and Thine eyes open, that Thou mayest hear the prayer of Thy servant, which I pray before Thee now, day and night, for the children of Israel Thy servants, and confess the sins of the children of Israel, which we have sinned against Thee: both I and my father's house have sinned. *Nehemiah 1:4,6*

Moreover Thou leddest them in the day by a cloudy pillar; and in the night by a pillar of fire, to give them light in the way wherein they should go.

Yet Thou in Thy manifold mercies forsookest them not in the wilderness: the pillar of the cloud departed not from them by day, to lead them in the way; neither the pillar of fire by night, to shew them light, and the way wherein they should go. *Nehemiah 9:12,19*

Thou shalt also decree a thing, and it shall be established unto thee: and the light shall shine upon thy ways.
Job 22:28

Teach me Thy way, O Lord, and lead me in a plain path, because of mine enemies. *Psalm 27:11*

I will instruct thee and teach thee in the way which thou shalt go: I will guide thee with Mine eye.   *Psalm 32:8*

For with Thee is the fountain of life: in Thy light shall we see light.
Psalm 36:9

O send out Thy light and Thy truth: let them lead me; let them bring me unto Thy holy hill, and to Thy tabernacles.   *Psalm 43:3*

So teach us to number our days, that we may apply our hearts unto wisdom.   *Psalm 90:12*

Unto the upright there ariseth light in the darkness: He is gracious, and full of compassion, and righteous.
Psalm 112:4

Thy word is a lamp unto my feet, and a light unto my path.
The entrance of Thy words giveth light; it giveth understanding unto the simple.   *Psalm 119:105,130*

Trust in the Lord with all thine

heart; and lean not unto thine own understanding.

In all thy ways acknowledge Him, and He shall direct thy paths.

Proverbs 3:5,6

The simple believeth every word: but the prudent man looketh well to his going. *Proverbs 14:15*

The spirit of man is the candle of the Lord, searching all the inward parts of the belly. *Proverbs 20:27*

A prudent man forseeth the evil, and hideth himself: but the simple pass on, and are punished. *Proverbs 22:3*

The Clearer Your Goal,
The Greater Your Faith.

-MIKE MURDOCK

∼ 54 ∼

WHEN YOU DESPERATELY NEED SOLITUDE OR QUIET TIME

Keep me as the apple of the eye, hide me under the shadow of Thy wings,   *Psalm 17:8*

He restoreth my soul: He leadeth me in the paths of righteousness for His name's sake.   *Psalm 23:3*

For in the time of trouble He shall hide me in His pavilion: in the secret of His tabernacle shall He hide me; He shall set me up upon a rock.
                    Psalm 27:5

Rest in the Lord, and wait patiently for Him: fret not thyself because of him who prospereth in his way, because of the man who bringeth wicked devices to pass.   *Psalm 37:7*

My heart panteth, my strength faileth me: as for the light of mine eyes, it also is gone from me.

For I am ready to halt, and my sorrow is continually before me.

Forsake me not, O Lord: O my God, be not far from me.

Make haste to help me, O Lord my salvation.   *Psalm 38:10,17,21,22*

Fearfulness and trembling are come upon me, and horror hath overwhelmed me.

And I said, Oh that I had wings like a dove! for then would I fly away, and be at rest.

Lo, then would I wander far off, and remain in the wilderness.

I would hasten my escape from the windy storm and tempest.

Psalm 55:5-8

Return unto thy rest, O my soul; for the Lord hath dealt bountifully with thee.

For Thou hast delivered my soul from death, mine eyes from tears, and my feet from falling.

I will walk before the Lord in the land of the living. *Psalm 116:7-9*

Come, My people, enter thou into thy chambers, and shut thy doors about thee: hide thyself as it were for a little moment, until the indignation be overpast. *Isaiah 26:20*

To whom He said, This is the rest wherewith ye may cause the weary to rest; and this is the refreshing: yet they would not hear. *Isaiah 28:12*

And My people shall dwell in a peaceable habitation, and in sure dwellings, and in quiet resting places;
Isaiah 32:18

Come unto Me, all ye that labour and are heavy laden, and I will give you rest.

Take My yoke upon you, and learn

of Me; for I am meek and lowly in heart: and ye shall find rest unto your souls.

Matthew 11:28,29

And He said unto them, Come ye yourselves apart into a desert place, and rest a while: for there were many coming and going, and they had no leisure so much as to eat.

And they departed into a desert place by ship privately.   *Mark 6:31,32*

There remaineth therefore a rest to the people of God.

For he that is entered into his rest, he also hath ceased from his own works, as God did from His.   *Hebrews 4:9,10*

Compassion Must Become
Your Seed
Before You Qualify
To Reap It
As Your Harvest.

-MIKE MURDOCK

YOUR STAFF

≈ 55 ≈

WHEN STAFF MEMBERS NEED SPECIAL ATTENTION

Moreover as for me, God forbid that I should sin against the Lord in ceasing to pray for you: but I will teach you the good and the right way:

1 Samuel 12:23

Then I told them of the hand of my God which was good upon me; as also the king's words that he had spoken unto me. And they said, Let us rise up and build. So they strengthened their hands for this good work.

Nehemiah 2:18

A brother offended is harder to be won than a strong city: and their contentions are like the bars of a castle.
Proverbs 18:19

He that rebuketh a man afterwards shall find more favour than he that flattereth with the tongue.
Proverbs 28:23

It is better to hear the rebuke of the wise, than for a man to hear the song of fools.   *Ecclesiastes 7:5*

Not slothful in business; fervent in spirit; serving the Lord;   *Romans 12:11*

For the scripture saith, Thou shalt not muzzle the ox that treadeth out the corn. And, The labourer is worthy of his reward.   *1 Timothy 5:18*

Wherefore I put thee in remembrance that thou stir up the gift of God, which is in thee by the putting on of my hands.   *2 Timothy 1:6*

Joy Is The Reward
For Recognizing
The Divine Product
Of The
Immediate Moment.

-MIKE MURDOCK

Every Success Provides
Portraits Of The Heart
Of Those Around You...
Joy In Your Friends,
Jealousy From Your Foes.

-MIKE MURDOCK

❧ 56 ❧

WHEN STAFF MEMBERS DEVELOP NEGATIVE ATTITUDES

━━━━━◆❖◆━━━━━

And thou, Solomon my son, know thou the God of thy father, and serve Him with a perfect heart and with a willing mind: for the Lord searcheth all hearts, and understandeth all the imaginations of the thoughts: if thou seek Him, He will be found of thee; but if thou forsake Him, He will cast thee off for ever. *1 Chronicles 28:9*

So built we the wall; and all the wall was joined together unto the half thereof: for the people had a mind to work. *Nehemiah 4:6*

Smite a scorner, and the simple

will beware: and reprove one that hath
understanding, and he will understand
knowledge.   *Proverbs 19:25*

When the scorner is punished, the
simple is made wise: and when the
wise is instructed, he receiveth
knowledge.   *Proverbs 21:11*

Open rebuke is better than secret
love.   *Proverbs 27:5*

It is better to hear the rebuke of
the wise, than for a man to hear the
song of fools.   *Ecclesiastes 7:5*

Thou wilt keep him in perfect
peace, whose mind is stayed on Thee:
because he trusteth in Thee.
                                Isaiah 26:3

And they come to Jesus, and see
him that was possessed with the devil,
and had the legion, sitting, and clothed,
and in his right mind: and they were
afraid.   *Mark 5:15*

Anything Small
Can Grow.

-MIKE MURDOCK

But speaking the truth in love, may grow up into Him in all things, which is the head, even Christ:

And be renewed in the spirit of your mind;   *Ephesians 4:15,23*

And have no fellowship with the unfruitful works of darkness, but rather reprove them.

But all things that are reproved are made manifest by the light: for whatsoever doth make manifest is light.   *Ephesians 5:11,13*

Fulfill ye my joy, that ye be likeminded, having the same love, being of one accord, of one mind.

Let this mind be in you, which was also in Christ Jesus:

Do all things without murmurings and disputings: *Philippians 2:2,5,14*

I beseech Euodias, and beseech Syntyche, that they be of the same mind in the Lord.   *Philippians 4:2*

But exhort one another daily, while

it is called To day; lest any of you be hardened through the deceitfulness of sin.   *Hebrews 3:13*

A double minded man is unstable in all his ways.   *James 1:8*

Wherefore gird up the loins of your mind, be sober, and hope to the end for the grace that is to be brought unto you at the revelation of Jesus Christ;
                                              1 Peter 1:13

The Instruction You Ignore...
Determines The Losses
You Experience.

-MIKE MURDOCK

≈ 57 ≈

WHEN STAFF MEMBERS NEGLECT THEIR DUTIES

▰▰●▰▰

My sons, be not now negligent: for the Lord hath chosen you to stand before Him, to serve Him, and that ye should minister unto Him, and burn incense. *2 Chronicles 29:11*

Take heed therefore unto yourselves, and to all the flock, over the which the Holy Ghost hath made you overseers, to feed the church of God, which He hath purchased with His own blood. *Acts 20:28*

Therefore seeing we have this ministry, as we have received mercy, we faint not; *2 Corinthians 4:1*

But have renounced the hidden things of dishonesty, not walking in craftiness, nor handling the word of God deceitfully; but by manifestation of the truth commending ourselves to every man's conscience in the sight of God.

But if our gospel be hid, it is hid to them that are lost:

In whom the god of this world hath blinded the minds of them which believe not, lest the light of the glorious gospel of Christ, Who is the image of God, should shine unto them.

For we preach not ourselves, but Christ Jesus the Lord; and ourselves your servants for Jesus' sake.

2 Corinthians 4:2-5

This charge I commit unto thee, son Timothy, according to the prophecies which went before on thee, that thou by them mightest war a good warfare;

Holding faith, and a good conscience; which some having put away concerning faith have made shipwreck: *1 Timothy 1:18,19*

These things command and teach.

Let no man despise thy youth; but be thou an example of the believers, in word, in conversation, in charity, in spirit, in faith, in purity.

Till I come, give attendance to reading, to exhortation, to doctrine.

Neglect not the gift that is in thee, which was given thee by prophecy, with the laying on of the hands of the presbytery.

Meditate upon these things; give thyself wholly to them; that thy profiting may appear to all.

Take heed unto thyself, and unto the doctrine; continue in them: for in doing this thou shalt both save thyself, and them that hear thee.

1 Timothy 4:11-16

Wherefore I put thee in remembrance that thou stir up the gift of God, which is in thee by the putting on of my hands.

For God hath not given us the spirit of fear; but of power, and of love, and of a sound mind.

Be not thou therefore ashamed of the testimony of our Lord, nor of me his prisoner: but be thou partaker of the afflictions of the gospel according to the power of God;   *2 Timothy 1:6-8*

Thou therefore, my son, be strong in the grace that is in Christ Jesus.

And the things that thou hast heard of me among many witnesses, the same commit thou to faithful men, who shall be able to teach others also.

Thou therefore endure hardness, as a good soldier of Jesus Christ.

No man that warreth entangleth himself with the affairs of this life; that he may please him who hath chosen him to be a soldier.

And if a man also strive for masteries, yet is he not crowned, except he strive lawfully.

The husbandman that laboureth must be first partaker of the fruits.

Consider what I say; and the Lord give thee understanding in all things.

Flee also youthful lusts: but follow righteousness, faith, charity, peace, with them that call on the Lord out of a pure heart.

But foolish and unlearned questions avoid, knowing that they do gender strifes.

And the servant of the Lord must not strive; but be gentle unto all men, apt to teach, patient,

2 Timothy 2:1-7,22-24

I charge thee therefore before God, and the Lord Jesus Christ, Who shall judge the quick and the dead at His appearing and His kingdom;

Preach the word; be instant in season, out of season; reprove, rebuke, exhort with all longsuffering and doctrine.

But watch thou in all things, endure afflictions, do the work of an evangelist, make full proof of thy ministry.   *2 Timothy 4:1,2,5*

And the Lord shall deliver me from every evil work, and will preserve me unto His heavenly kingdom: to Whom be glory for ever and ever. Amen.

2 Timothy 4:18

What You Can Tolerate
You Cannot Change.

-MIKE MURDOCK

≈ 58 ≈

WHEN STAFF MEMBERS NEED ENCOURAGEMENT TOWARD EXCELLENCE

But Joshua the son of Nun, which standeth before thee, he shall go in thither: encourage him: for he shall cause Israel to inherit it.

Deuteronomy 1:38

But charge Joshua, and encourage him, and strengthen him: for he shall go over before this people, and he shall cause them to inherit the land which thou shalt see.   *Deuteronomy 3:28*

And the people the men of Israel encouraged themselves, and set their battle again in array in the place where they put themselves in array the first day.   *Judges 20:22*

And David was greatly distressed;
for the people spake of stoning him,
because the soul of all the people was
grieved, every man for his sons and for
his daughters: but David encouraged
himself in the Lord his God.

1 Samuel 30:6

And he set the priests in their
charges, and encouraged them to the
service of the house of the Lord,

2 Chronicles 35:2

Thy God hath commanded Thy
strength: strengthen, O God, that which
Thou hast wrought for us. *Psalm 68:28*

In the day when I cried Thou
answeredst me, and strengthenedst me
with strength in my soul. *Psalm 138:3*

O Lord, Thou hast searched me,
and known me.

Thou knowest my downsitting and
mine uprising, Thou understandest my
thought afar off.

Thou compassest my path and my

lying down, and art acquainted with all my ways.

For there is not a word in my tongue, but, lo, O Lord, Thou knowest it altogether.

Thou hast beset me behind and before, and laid Thine hand upon me.

Psalm 139:1-5

Wisdom strengtheneth the wise more than ten mighty men which are in the city.   *Ecclesiastes 7:19*

So the carpenter encouraged the goldsmith, and he that smootheth with the hammer him that smote the anvil, saying, It is ready for the sodering: and he fastened it with nails, that it should not be moved.   *Isaiah 41:7*

And unto one He gave five talents, to another two, and to another one; to every man according to his several ability; and straightway took His journey.

For unto every one that hath shall be given, and he shall have abundance: but from him that hath not shall be

taken away even that which he hath.
Matthew 25:15,29

But I have prayed for thee, that
thy faith fail not: and when thou art
converted, strengthen thy brethren.
Luke 22:32

And, behold, I send the promise of
my Father upon you: but tarry ye in the
city of Jerusalem, until ye be endued
with power from on high.   *Luke 24:49*

But ye shall receive power, after
that the Holy Ghost is come upon you:
and ye shall be witnesses unto Me both
in Jerusalem, and in all Judaea, and in
Samaria, and unto the uttermost part
of the earth.   *Acts 1:8*

And immediately there fell from
his eyes as it had been scales: and he
received sight forthwith, and arose, and
was baptized.
And when he had received meat,
he was strengthened. Then was Saul
certain days with the disciples which

were at Damascus.

And straightway he preached Christ in the synagogues, that He is the Son of God.

But all that heard him were amazed, and said; Is not this he that destroyed them which called on this name in Jerusalem, and came hither for that intent, that he might bring them bound unto the chief priests?

But Saul increased the more in strength, and confounded the Jews which dwelt at Damascus, proving that this is very Christ.   *Acts 9:18-22*

That He would grant you, according to the riches of His glory, to be strengthened with might by His Spirit in the inner man;

Ephesians 3:16

Strengthened with all might, according to His glorious power, unto all patience and longsuffering with joyfulness;   *Colossians 1:11*

I can do all things through Christ

which strengtheneth me.

Philippians 4:13

But the God of all grace, Who hath
called us unto His eternal glory by
Christ Jesus, after that ye have
suffered a while, make you perfect,
stablish, strengthen, settle you.

1 Peter 5:10

Remember therefore how thou
hast received and heard, and hold fast,
and repent. If therefore thou shalt not
watch, I will come on thee as a thief,
and thou shalt not know what hour I
will come upon thee.   *Revelation 3:3*

❧ 59 ❧

WHEN YOU MUST RELEASE A KEY STAFF MEMBER

And Abram said unto Lot, Let there be no strife, I pray thee, between me and thee, and between my herdmen and thy herdmen; for we be brethren.

And Lot lifted up his eyes, and beheld all the plain of Jordan, that it was well watered every where, before the Lord destroyed Sodom and Gomorrah, even as the garden of the Lord, like the land of Egypt, as thou comest unto Zoar.

Then Lot chose him all the plain of Jordan; and Lot journeyed east: and they separated themselves the one from the other.

And the Lord said unto Abram,

after that Lot was separated from him,
Lift up now thine eyes, and look from
the place where thou art northward,
and southward, and eastward, and
westward:

For all the land which thou seest,
to thee will I give it, and to thy seed for
ever.

And I will make thy seed as the
dust of the earth: so that if a man can
number the dust of the earth, then shall
thy seed also be numbered.

Arise, walk through the land in the
length of it and in the breadth of it; for
I will give it unto thee.

Genesis 13:8,10,11,14-17

The Lord lift up His countenance
upon thee, and give thee peace.

Numbers 6:26

For the Lord thy God is a merciful
God; He will not forsake thee, neither
destroy thee, nor forget the covenant of
thy fathers which He sware unto them.

Deuteronomy 4:31

Be strong and of a good courage,
fear not, nor be afraid of them: for the
Lord thy God, He it is that doth go with
thee; He will not fail thee, nor forsake
thee.

And Moses called unto Joshua, and
said unto him in the sight of all Israel,
Be strong and of a good courage: for
thou must go with this people unto the
land which the Lord hath sworn unto
their fathers to give them; and thou
shalt cause them to inherit it.

And the Lord, He it is that doth go
before thee; He will be with thee, He
will not fail thee, neither forsake thee:
fear not, neither be dismayed.

Deuteronomy 31:6-8

The eternal God is thy refuge, and
underneath are the everlasting arms:
and He shall thrust out the enemy from
before thee; and shall say, Destroy
them.   *Deuteronomy 33:27*

I had fainted, unless I had believed
to see the goodness of the Lord in the
land of the living.

Wait on the Lord: be of good courage, and He shall strengthen thine heart: wait, I say, on the Lord.

Psalm 27:13,14

Make Thy face to shine upon Thy servant: save me for Thy mercies' sake.

Psalm 31:16

Now the God of hope fill you with all joy and peace in believing, that ye may abound in hope, through the power of the Holy Ghost. *Romans 15:13*

And did all eat the same spiritual meat; *1 Corinthians 10:3*

But the fruit of the Spirit is love, joy, peace, longsuffering, gentleness, goodness, faith, *Galatians 5:22*

Finally, my brethren, be strong in the Lord, and in the power of His might.

Ephesians 6:10

And I intreat thee also, true yokefellow, help those women which laboured with me in the gospel, with

Clement also, and with other my fellow labourers, whose names are in the book of life. *Philippians 4:3*

Not that I speak in respect of want: for I have learned, in whatsoever state I am, therewith to be content.
I know both how to be abased, and I know how to abound: every where and in all things I am instructed both to be full and to be hungry, both to abound and to suffer need. *Philippians 4:11,12*

Let your conversation be without covetousness; and be content with such things as ye have: for He hath said, I will never leave thee, nor forsake thee.
Hebrews 13:5

That the trial of your faith, being much more precious than of gold that perisheth, though it be tried with fire, might be found unto praise and honour and glory at the appearing of Jesus Christ: *1 Peter 1:7*

Casting all your care upon Him; for He careth for you. *1 Peter 5:7*

∽ 60 ∽

WHEN A KEY STAFF MEMBER LEAVES YOU FOR ANOTHER MINISTRY

The Lord shall fight for you, and ye shall hold your peace. *Exodus 14:14*

The eternal God is thy refuge, and underneath are the everlasting arms: and He shall thrust out the enemy from before thee; and shall say, Destroy them. *Deuteronomy 33:27*

I would seek unto God, and unto God would I commit my cause:
Which doeth great things and unsearchable; marvellous things without number:
Who giveth rain upon the earth, and sendeth waters upon the fields:
Job 5:8-10

In my distress I called upon the Lord, and cried unto my God: He heard my voice out of His temple, and my cry came before Him, even into His ears.

Psalm 18:6

The steps of a good man are ordered by the Lord: and He delighteth in his way.

Though he fall, he shall not be utterly cast down: for the Lord upholdeth him with His hand.

Psalm 37:23,24

Be still, and know that I am God: I will be exalted among the heathen, I will be exalted in the earth.

Psalm 46:10

When thou passest through the waters, I will be with thee; and through the rivers, they shall not overflow thee: when thou walkest through the fire, thou shalt not be burned; neither shall the flame kindle upon thee. *Isaiah 43:2*

Woe is me for my hurt! my wound

is grievous: but I said, Truly this is a grief, and I must bear it.

Jeremiah 10:19

When my soul fainted within me I remembered the Lord: and my prayer came in unto Thee, into Thine holy temple.

But I will sacrifice unto Thee with the voice of thanksgiving; I will pay that that I have vowed. Salvation is of the Lord.

Jonah 2:7,9

The Lord is good, a strong hold in the day of trouble; and He knoweth them that trust in Him.

Nahum 1:7

And we are witnesses of all things which He did both in the land of the Jews, and in Jerusalem; Whom they slew and hanged on a tree:

Him God raised up the third day, and shewed Him openly; *Acts 10:39,40*

And when he would not be persuaded, we ceased, saying, The will of the Lord be done.

Acts 21:14

❧ 61 ❧

WHEN A KEY STAFF MEMBER LACKS PASSION

For there is hope of a tree, if it be cut down, that it will sprout again, and that the tender branch thereof will not cease. *Job 14:7*

But they that wait upon the Lord shall renew their strength; they shall mount up with wings as eagles; they shall run, and not be weary; and they shall walk, and not faint. *Isaiah 40:31*

For I will pour water upon him that is thirsty, and floods upon the dry ground: I will pour My spirit upon thy seed, and My blessing upon thine offspring: *Isaiah 44:3*

For we are labourers together with God: ye are God's husbandry, ye are God's building. *1 Corinthians 3:9*

Champions Walk Away From
Something They Desire
To Protect Something Else
They Love.

-MIKE MURDOCK

YOUR FAMILY

❧ 62 ❧

WHEN CHURCH DUTIES THREATEN TO ROB YOU OF IMPORTANT FAMILY TIME

For I know him, that he will command his children and his household after him, and they shall keep the way of the Lord, to do justice and judgment; that the Lord may bring upon Abraham that which he hath spoken of him.   *Genesis 18:19*

Only take heed to thyself, and keep thy soul diligently, lest thou forget the things which thine eyes have seen, and lest they depart from thy heart all the days of thy life: but teach them thy sons, and thy sons' sons;

Deuteronomy 4:9

And thou shalt teach them diligently unto thy children, and shalt talk of them when thou sittest in thine house, and when thou walkest by the way, and when thou liest down, and when thou risest up.   *Deuteronomy 6:7*

And if it seem evil unto you to serve the Lord, choose you this day whom ye will serve; whether the gods which your fathers served that were on the other side of the flood, or the gods of the Amorites, in whose land ye shall dwell: but as for me and my house, we will serve the Lord.   *Joshua 24:15*

For I have told him that I will judge his house for ever for the iniquity which he knoweth; because his sons made themselves vile, and he restrained them not.   *1 Samuel 3:13*

And his sons walked not in his ways, but turned aside after lucre, and took bribes, and perverted judgment.

1 Samuel 8:3

And his father had not displeased him at any time in saying, Why hast thou done so? and he also was a very goodly man; and his mother bare him after Absalom. *1 Kings 1:6*

For He established a testimony in Jacob, and appointed a law in Israel, which He commanded our fathers, that they should make them known to their children:

That the generation to come might know them, even the children which should be born; who should arise and declare them to their children:

Psalm 78:5,6

Lo, children are an heritage of the Lord: and the fruit of the womb is His reward.

As arrows are in the hand of a mighty man; so are children of the youth. *Psalm 127:3,4*

Happy is the man that hath his quiver full of them: they shall not be ashamed, but they shall speak with the enemies in the gate.   *Psalm 127:5*

A soft answer turneth away wrath: but grievous words stir up anger.
                        Proverbs 15:1

Train up a child in the way he should go: and when he is old, he will not depart from it.   *Proverbs 22:6*

The rod and reproof give wisdom: but a child left to himself bringeth his mother to shame.   *Proverbs 29:15*

And the Lord saith, Because they have forsaken My law which I set before them, and have not obeyed My voice, neither walked therein;
But have walked after the imagination of their own heart, and after Baalim, which their fathers taught them: *Jeremiah 9:13,14*

Tell ye your children of it, and let your children tell their children, and their children another generation.

Joel 1:3

If ye then, being evil, know how to give good gifts unto your children, how much more shall your Father which is in heaven give good things to them that ask Him? *Matthew 7:11*

If ye then, being evil, know how to give good gifts unto your children: how much more shall your heavenly Father give the Holy Spirit to them that ask him? *Luke 11:13*

So when they had dined, Jesus saith to Simon Peter, Simon, son of Jonas, lovest thou Me more than these? He saith unto Him, Yea, Lord; Thou knowest that I love Thee. He saith unto him, Feed My lambs. *John 21:15*

So ought men to love their wives as their own bodies. He that loveth his wife loveth himself.

Nevertheless let every one of you in particular so love his wife even as himself; and the wife see that she reverence her husband.

Ephesians 5:28,33

And, ye fathers, provoke not your children to wrath: but bring them up in the nurture and admonition of the Lord. *Ephesians 6:4*

Husbands, love your wives, and be not bitter against them.

Fathers, provoke not your children to anger, lest they be discouraged.

Colossians 3:19,21

Likewise, ye husbands, dwell with them according to knowledge, giving honour unto the wife, as unto the weaker vessel, and as being heirs together of the grace of life; that your prayers be not hindered. *1 Peter 3:7*

∾ 63 ∾

WHEN YOUR SPOUSE
SEEMS UNSUPPORTIVE

Hatred stirreth up strifes: but love covereth all sins. *Proverbs 10:12*

Only by pride cometh contention: but with the well advised is wisdom.
Proverbs 13:10

A soft answer turneth away wrath: but grievous words stir up anger.

A wrathful man stirreth up strife: but he that is slow to anger appeaseth strife.

A man hath joy by the answer of his mouth: and a word spoken in due season, how good is it!
Proverbs 15:1,18,23

He loveth transgression that

loveth strife: and he that exalteth his
gate seeketh destruction.

Proverbs 17:19

A fool's lips enter into contention,
and his mouth calleth for strokes.

Proverbs 18:6

The discretion of a man deferreth
his anger; and it is his glory to pass over
a transgression.   *Proverbs 19:11*

It is an honour for a man to cease
from strife: but every fool will be
meddling.   *Proverbs 20:3*

But I say unto you, That ye resist
not evil: but whosoever shall smite thee
on thy right cheek, turn to him the
other also.

And if any man will sue thee at the
law, and take away thy coat, let him
have thy cloak also.

And whosoever shall compel thee
to go a mile, go with him twain.

Give to him that asketh thee, and
from him that would borrow of thee
turn not thou away.   *Matthew 5:39-42*

Wherefore they are no more twain, but one flesh. What therefore God hath joined together, let not man put asunder. *Matthew 19:6*

And if a house be divided against itself, that house cannot stand.
Mark 3:25

If it be possible, as much as lieth in you, live peaceably with all men.
Romans 12:18

Wives, submit yourselves unto your own husbands, as it is fit in the Lord.

Husbands, love your wives, and be not bitter against them.
Colossians 3:18,19

But if any provide not for his own, and specially for those of his own house, he hath denied the faith, and is worse than an infidel. *1 Timothy 5:8*

But if ye have bitter envying and strife in your hearts, glory not, and lie not against the truth.

This wisdom descendeth not from above, but is earthly, sensual, devilish.

For where envying and strife is, there is confusion and every evil work.

But the wisdom that is from above is first pure, then peaceable, gentle, and easy to be intreated, full of mercy and good fruits, without partiality, and without hypocrisy.   *James 3:14-17*

From whence come wars and fightings among you? come they not hence, even of your lusts that war in your members?

Ye lust, and have not: ye kill, and desire to have, and cannot obtain: ye fight and war, yet ye have not, because ye ask not.

Ye ask, and receive not, because ye ask amiss, that ye may consume it upon your lusts.   *James 4:1-3*

Likewise, ye husbands, dwell with them according to knowledge, giving honour unto the wife, as unto the weaker vessel, and as being heirs together of the grace of life; that your prayers be not hindered.   *1 Peter 3:7*

Satan's Favorite Entry Point
Into Your Life
Is Always Through Someone
Close To You.

-MIKE MURDOCK

≈ 64 ≈

WHEN YOUR SPOUSE FEELS UNAPPRECIATED

And the Lord God said, It is not good that the man should be alone; I will make him an help meet for him.

And Adam said, This is now bone of my bones, and flesh of my flesh: she shall be called Woman, because she was taken out of Man.

Therefore shall a man leave his father and his mother, and shall cleave unto his wife: and they shall be one flesh.   *Genesis 2:18,23,24*

When a man hath taken a new wife, he shall not go out to war, neither shall he be charged with any business: but he shall be free at home one year, and shall cheer up his wife which he hath taken.   *Deuteronomy 24:5*

Let thy fountain be blessed: and rejoice with the wife of thy youth.

Let her be as the loving hind and pleasant roe; let her breasts satisfy thee at all times; and be thou ravished always with her love. *Proverbs 5:18,19*

The righteousness of the upright shall deliver them: but transgressors shall be taken in their own naughtiness.

A gracious woman retaineth honour: and strong men retain riches.
Proverbs 11:6,16

The hand of the diligent shall bear rule: but the slothful shall be under tribute. *Proverbs 12:24*

Every wise woman buildeth her house: but the foolish plucketh it down with her hands. *Proverbs 14:1*

Whoso findeth a wife findeth a good thing, and obtaineth favour of the Lord. *Proverbs 18:22*

House and riches are the inheritance of fathers: and a prudent wife is from the Lord.   *Proverbs 19:14*

Who can find a virtuous woman? for her price is far above rubies.

The heart of her husband doth safely trust in her, so that he shall have no need of spoil.

She will do him good and not evil all the days of her life.

Proverbs 31:10-12

Live joyfully with the wife whom thou lovest all the days of the life of thy vanity, which He hath given thee under the sun, all the days of thy vanity: for that is thy portion in this life, and in thy labour which thou takest under the sun.   *Ecclesiastes 9:9*

And did not he make one? Yet had he the residue of the spirit. And wherefore one? That he might seek a godly seed. Therefore take heed to your spirit, and let none deal treacherously against the wife of his youth.

For the Lord, the God of Israel, saith that he hateth putting away: for one covereth violence with his garment, saith the Lord of hosts: therefore take heed to your spirit, that ye deal not treacherously.   *Malachi 2:15,16*

Let the husband render unto the wife due benevolence: and likewise also the wife unto the husband.

The wife hath not power of her own body, but the husband: and likewise also the husband hath not power of his own body, but the wife.

Defraud ye not one the other, except it be with consent for a time, that ye may give yourselves to fasting and prayer; and come together again, that satan tempt you not for your incontinency.

But he that is married careth for the things that are of the world, how he may please his wife.

1 Corinthians 7:3-5,33

Nevertheless neither is the man without the woman, neither the woman without the man, in the Lord.

For as the woman is of the man, even so is the man also by the woman; but all things of God.

1 Corinthians 11:11,12

Husbands, love your wives, even as Christ also loved the church, and gave Himself for it;

That He might sanctify and cleanse it with the washing of water by the word,

That He might present it to Himself a glorious church, not having spot, or wrinkle, or any such thing; but that it should be holy and without blemish.

So ought men to love their wives as their own bodies. He that loveth his wife loveth himself.

For no man ever yet hated his own flesh; but nourisheth and cherisheth it, even as the Lord the church:

Nevertheless let every one of you in particular so love his wife even as himself; and the wife see that she reverence her husband.

Ephesians 5:25-29,33

Husbands, love your wives, and be not bitter against them.

Colossians 3:19

But if any provide not for his own, and specially for those of his own house, he hath denied the faith, and is worse than an infidel.   *1 Timothy 5:8*

Likewise, ye husbands, dwell with them according to knowledge, giving honour unto the wife, as unto the weaker vessel, and as being heirs together of the grace of life; that your prayers be not hindered.   *1 Peter 3:7*

≈ 65 ≈

WHEN YOU FACE CONTINUAL MARITAL CONFLICT

And He arose, and rebuked the wind, and said unto the sea, Peace, be still. And the wind ceased, and there was a great calm.   *Mark 4:39*

And as they thus spake, Jesus Himself stood in the midst of them, and saith unto them, Peace be unto you.

Luke 24:36

The thief cometh not, but for to steal, and to kill, and to destroy: I am come that they might have life, and that they might have it more abundantly.

John 10:10

Peace I leave with you, My peace I give unto you: not as the world giveth, give I unto you. Let not your heart be troubled, neither let it be afraid.

John 14:27

These things I have spoken unto you, that in Me ye might have peace. In the world ye shall have tribulation: but be of good cheer; I have overcome the world. *John 16:33*

Then the same day at evening, being the first day of the week, when the doors were shut where the disciples were assembled for fear of the Jews, came Jesus and stood in the midst, and saith unto them, Peace be unto you.

John 20:19

And when they had laid many stripes upon them, they cast them into prison, charging the jailor to keep them safely:

Who, having received such a charge, thrust them into the inner prison, and made their feet fast in the stocks.

And at midnight Paul and Silas prayed, and sang praises unto God: and the prisoners heard them. *Acts 16:23-25*

For to be carnally minded is death; but to be spiritually minded is life and peace. *Romans 8:6*

Now the God of hope fill you with all joy and peace in believing, that ye may abound in hope, through the power of the Holy Ghost. *Romans 15:13*

And the God of peace shall bruise satan under your feet shortly. The grace of our Lord Jesus Christ be with you. Amen. *Romans 16:20*

Grace be unto you, and peace, from God our Father, and from the Lord Jesus Christ. *1 Corinthians 1:3*

Now we have received, not the spirit of the world, but the spirit which is of God; that we might know the things that are freely given to us of God. *1 Corinthians 2:12*

Finally, brethren, farewell. Be perfect, be of good comfort, be of one mind, live in peace; and the God of love and peace shall be with you.

2 Corinthians 13:11

That He would grant you, according to the riches of His glory, to be strengthened with might by His Spirit in the inner man;

And to know the love of Christ, which passeth knowledge, that ye might be filled with all the fulness of God. *Ephesians 3:16,19*

Finally, my brethren, be strong in the Lord, and in the power of His might.

Ephesians 6:10

Even as it is meet for me to think this of you all, because I have you in my heart; inasmuch as both in my bonds, and in the defence and confirmation of the gospel, ye all are partakers of my grace. *Philippians 1:7*

We give thanks to God and the

Father of our Lord Jesus Christ,
praying always for you,

For this cause we also, since the
day we heard it, do not cease to pray for
you, and to desire that ye might be
filled with the knowledge of His will in
all wisdom and spiritual understanding;

That ye might walk worthy of the
Lord unto all pleasing, being fruitful in
every good work, and increasing in the
knowledge of God;

Strengthened with all might,
according to His glorious power, unto all
patience and longsuffering with
joyfulness; *Colossians 1:3,9-11*

And the very God of peace sanctify
you wholly; and I pray God your whole
spirit and soul and body be preserved
blameless unto the coming of our Lord
Jesus Christ. *1 Thessalonians 5:23*

Now the Lord of peace Himself
give you peace always by all means.
The Lord be with you all.
2 Thessalonians 3:16

Now the God of peace, that brought again from the dead our Lord Jesus, that great shepherd of the sheep, through the blood of the everlasting covenant,

Make you perfect in every good work to do His will, working in you that which is wellpleasing in His sight, through Jesus Christ; to Whom be glory for ever and ever. Amen.

Hebrews 13:20,21

Elias was a man subject to like passions as we are, and he prayed earnestly that it might not rain: and it rained not on the earth by the space of three years and six months.

And he prayed again, and the heaven gave rain, and the earth brought forth her fruit. *James 5:17,18*

God Speaks Two Ways:
People And Pain.

-MIKE MURDOCK

≈ 66 ≈

WHEN YOUR CHILDREN BECOME REBELLIOUS

Be ye strong therefore, and let not your hands be weak: for your work shall be rewarded.   *2 Chronicles 15:7*

And they rose early in the morning, and went forth into the wilderness of Tekoa: and as they went forth, Jehoshaphat stood and said, Hear me, O Judah, and ye inhabitants of Jerusalem; Believe in the Lord your God, so shall ye be established; believe His prophets, so shall ye prosper.
2 Chronicles 20:20

The Lord also will be a refuge for the oppressed, a refuge in times of trouble.

And they that know Thy name will put their trust in Thee: for Thou, Lord,

hast not forsaken them that seek Thee.
Psalm 9:9,10

Many sorrows shall be to the
wicked: but he that trusteth in the
Lord, mercy shall compass him about.
Psalm 32:10

Trust in the Lord with all thine
heart; and lean not unto thine own
understanding. *Proverbs 3:5*

He that is of a proud heart stirreth
up strife: but he that putteth his trust
in the Lord shall be made fat.
Proverbs 28:25

Thou wilt keep him in perfect
peace, whose mind is stayed on Thee:
because he trusteth in Thee.
Isaiah 26:3

Blessed is the man that trusteth in
the Lord, and whose hope the Lord is.

For he shall be as a tree planted by
the waters, and that spreadeth out her
roots by the river, and shall not see
when heat cometh, but her leaf shall be

green; and shall not be careful in the year of drought, neither shall cease from yielding fruit. *Jeremiah 17:7,8*

Jesus answered and said unto them, Verily I say unto you, If ye have faith, and doubt not, ye shall not only do this which is done to the fig tree, but also if ye shall say unto this mountain, Be thou removed, and be thou cast into the sea; it shall be done.

And all things, whatsoever ye shall ask in prayer, believing, ye shall receive. *Matthew 21:21,22*

Jesus said unto him, If thou canst believe, all things are possible to him that believeth. *Mark 9:23*

Therefore I say unto you, What things soever ye desire, when ye pray, believe that ye receive them, and ye shall have them. *Mark 11:24*

For what saith the scripture? Abraham believed God, and it was counted unto him for righteousness.

Who against hope believed in hope,

that he might become the father of many nations; according to that which was spoken, So shall thy seed be.

And being not weak in faith, he considered not his own body now dead, when he was about an hundred years old, neither yet the deadness of Sarah's womb:

He staggered not at the promise of God through unbelief; but was strong in faith, giving glory to God;

And being fully persuaded that, what He had promised, He was able also to perform.   *Romans 4:3,18-21*

Now the God of hope fill you with all joy and peace in believing, that ye may abound in hope, through the power of the Holy Ghost.   *Romans 15:13*

And, ye fathers, provoke not your children to wrath: but bring them up in the nurture and admonition of the Lord.   *Ephesians 6:4*

Cast not away therefore your confidence, which hath great recompence of reward.   *Hebrews 10:35*

Change Is
Always Proportionate
To Knowledge.

-MIKE MURDOCK

❧ 67 ❧

WHEN YOUR CHILDREN SEEM INDIFFERENT TO YOUR MINISTRY

Thou shalt also decree a thing, and it shall be established unto thee: and the light shall shine upon thy ways.

When men are cast down, then thou shalt say, There is lifting up; and He shall save the humble person.

Job 22:28,29

For Thou wilt light my candle: the Lord my God will enlighten my darkness. *Psalm 18:28*

My foot standeth in an even place: in the congregations will I bless the Lord. *Psalm 26:12*

Let not the foot of pride come

against me, and let not the hand of the wicked remove me. *Psalm 36:11*

And He shall bring forth Thy righteousness as the light, and Thy judgment as the noonday.

Rest in the Lord, and wait patiently for Him: fret not thyself because of him who prospereth in his way, because of the man who bringeth wicked devices to pass. *Psalm 37:6,7*

Through Thee will we push down our enemies: through Thy name will we tread them under that rise up against us. *Psalm 44:5*

For He shall give His angels charge over thee, to keep thee in all thy ways.

They shall bear thee up in their hands, lest thou dash thy foot against a stone. *Psalm 91:11,12*

I will lift up mine eyes unto the hills, from whence cometh my help.

My help cometh from the Lord, which made heaven and earth.

He will not suffer thy foot to be moved: He that keepeth thee will not slumber.   *Psalm 121:1-3*

Hear me speedily, O Lord: my spirit faileth: hide not Thy face from me, lest I be like unto them that go down into the pit.   *Psalm 143:7*

Blessed are ye, when men shall revile you, and persecute you, and shall say all manner of evil against you falsely, for My sake.   *Matthew 5:11*

And the brother shall deliver up the brother to death, and the father the child: and the children shall rise up against their parents, and cause them to be put to death.

And ye shall be hated of all men for My name's sake: but he that endureth to the end shall be saved.

And a man's foes shall be they of his own household.

Matthew 10:21,22,36

Behold, I give unto you power to tread on serpents and scorpions, and

over all the power of the enemy: and
nothing shall by any means hurt you.

Luke 10:19

I speak not of you all: I know
whom I have chosen: but that the
scripture may be fulfilled, He that
eateth bread with Me hath lifted up his
heel against Me.

Now I tell you before it come, that,
when it is come to pass, ye may believe
that I am He.

Verily, verily, I say unto you, He
that receiveth whomsoever I send
receiveth Me; and he that receiveth Me
receiveth Him that sent Me.

John 13:18-20

And the God of peace shall bruise
satan under your feet shortly. The
grace of our Lord Jesus Christ be with
you. Amen. *Romans 16:20*

And God is able to make all grace
abound toward you; that ye, always
having all sufficiency in all things, may
abound to every good work:

2 Corinthians 9:8

And He said unto me, My grace is sufficient for thee: for My strength is made perfect in weakness. Most gladly therefore will I rather glory in my infirmities, that the power of Christ may rest upon me. *2 Corinthians 12:9*

My little children, let us not love in word, neither in tongue; but in deed and in truth.

And hereby we know that we are of the truth, and shall assure our hearts before Him.

For if our heart condemn us, God is greater than our heart, and knoweth all things.

Beloved, if our heart condemn us not, then have we confidence toward God.

And whatsoever we ask, we receive of Him, because we keep His commandments, and do those things that are pleasing in His sight. *1 John 3:18-22*

And this commandment have we from Him, That he who loveth God love his brother also. *1 John 4:21*

❧ 68 ❧

WHEN YOUR CHILDREN RESENT THE TIME YOU SPEND WITH OTHERS

The liberal soul shall be made fat: and he that watereth shall be watered also himself.   *Proverbs 11:25*

Is not this the fast that I have chosen? to loose the bands of wickedness, to undo the heavy burdens, and to let the oppressed go free, and that ye break every yoke?

Is it not to deal thy bread to the hungry, and that thou bring the poor that are cast out to thy house? when thou seest the naked, that thou cover him; and that thou hide not thyself from thine own flesh?

Then shall thy light break forth as

the morning, and thine health shall
spring forth speedily: and thy righteousness shall go before thee; the glory
of the Lord shall be thy reward.

Then shalt thou call, and the Lord
shall answer; thou shalt cry, and He
shall say, Here I am. If thou take away
from the midst of thee the yoke, the
putting forth of the finger, and speaking
vanity; *Isaiah 58:6-9*

He hath shewed thee, O man, what
is good; and what doth the Lord require
of thee, but to do justly, and to love
mercy, and to walk humbly with thy
God? *Micah 6:8*

Blessed are the merciful: for they
shall obtain mercy.

Blessed are the pure in heart: for
they shall see God.

Blessed are the peacemakers: for
they shall be called the children of God.
Matthew 5:7-9

Therefore all things whatsoever ye
would that men should do to you, do ye

even so to them: for this is the law and the prophets. *Matthew 7:12*

Then shall the King say unto them on His right hand, Come, ye blessed of My Father, inherit the kingdom prepared for you from the foundation of the world:

For I was an hungred, and ye gave Me meat: I was thirsty, and ye gave Me drink: I was a stranger, and ye took Me in:

Naked, and ye clothed Me: I was sick, and ye visited Me: I was in prison, and ye came unto Me. *Matthew 25:34-36*

For whosoever shall give you a cup of water to drink in My name, because ye belong to Christ, verily I say unto you, he shall not lose his reward. *Mark 9:41*

Be ye therefore merciful, as your Father also is merciful. *Luke 6:36*

But a certain Samaritan, as he journeyed, came where he was: and

when he saw him, he had compassion
on him,   *Luke 10:33*

Blessed be God, even the Father of
our Lord Jesus Christ, the Father of
mercies, and the God of all comfort;
Who comforteth us in all our
tribulation, that we may be able to
comfort them which are in any trouble,
by the comfort wherewith we ourselves
are comforted of God.
For as the sufferings of Christ
abound in us, so our consolation also
aboundeth by Christ.
And whether we be afflicted, it is
for your consolation and salvation,
which is effectual in the enduring of the
same sufferings which we also suffer:
or whether we be comforted, it is for
your consolation and salvation.
                    2 Corinthians 1:3-6

Put on therefore, as the elect of
God, holy and beloved, bowels of
mercies, kindness, humbleness of mind,
meekness, longsuffering;
                    Colossians 3:12

YOUR FINANCES

∼ 69 ∼

WHEN YOUR SALARY SEEMS INADEQUATE

━━━━►◦◄━━━━

And it shall come to pass, if thou shalt hearken diligently unto the voice of the Lord thy God, to observe and to do all His commandments which I command thee this day, that the Lord thy God will set thee on high above all nations of the earth:

And all these blessings shall come on thee, and overtake thee, if thou shalt hearken unto the voice of the Lord thy God.

Blessed shalt thou be in the city, and blessed shalt thou be in the field.

Blessed shall be the fruit of thy

body, and the fruit of thy ground, and
the fruit of thy cattle, the increase of
thy kine, and the flocks of thy sheep.

Deuteronomy 28:1-4

The Lord is my shepherd; I shall
not want. *Psalm 23:1*

The steps of a good man are
ordered by the Lord: and He delighteth
in his way.

Though he fall, he shall not be
utterly cast down: for the Lord
upholdeth him with His hand.

I have been young, and now am
old; yet have I not seen the righteous
forsaken, nor His seed begging bread.

Psalm 37:23-25

He will regard the prayer of the
destitute, and not despise their prayer.

Psalm 102:17

Remove far from me vanity and
lies: give me neither poverty nor riches;
feed me with food convenient for me:

Lest I be full, and deny thee, and

say, Who is the Lord? or lest I be poor,
and steal, and take the name of my God
in vain.   *Proverbs 30:8,9*

Fear thou not; for I am with thee:
be not dismayed; for I am thy God: I
will strengthen thee; yea, I will help
thee; yea, I will uphold thee with the
right hand of My righteousness.
For I the Lord thy God will hold
thy right hand, saying unto thee, Fear
not; I will help thee.
Fear not, thou worm Jacob, and ye
men of Israel; I will help thee, saith the
Lord, and thy redeemer, the Holy One of
Israel.
When the poor and needy seek
water, and there is none, and their
tongue faileth for thirst, I the Lord will
hear them, I the God of Israel will not
forsake them.   *Isaiah 41:10,13,14,17*

Although the fig tree shall not
blossom, neither shall fruit be in the
vines; the labour of the olive shall fail,
and the fields shall yield no meat; the
flock shall be cut off from the fold, and

there shall be no herd in the stalls:

Yet I will rejoice in the Lord, I will joy in the God of my salvation.

Habakkuk 3:17,18

Therefore I say unto you, Take no thought for your life, what ye shall eat, or what ye shall drink; nor yet for your body, what ye shall put on. Is not the life more than meat, and the body than raiment?

Wherefore, if God so clothe the grass of the field, which to day is, and to morrow is cast into the oven, shall He not much more clothe you, O ye of little faith?

But seek ye first the kingdom of God, and His righteousness; and all these things shall be added unto you.

Take therefore no thought for the morrow: for the morrow shall take thought for the things of itself. Sufficient unto the day is the evil thereof.   *Matthew 6:25,30,33,34*

Give, and it shall be given unto you; good measure, pressed down, and shaken together, and running over, shall men give into your bosom. For with the same measure that ye mete withal it shall be measured to you again.   *Luke 6:38*

For it is written in the law of Moses, Thou shalt not muzzle the mouth of the ox that treadeth out the corn. Doth God take care for oxen?

Or saith he it altogether for our sakes? For our sakes, no doubt, this is written: that he that ploweth should plow in hope; and that he that thresheth in hope should be partaker of his hope.   *1 Corinthians 9:9,10*

I know both how to be abased, and I know how to abound: every where and in all things I am instructed both to be full and to be hungry, both to abound and to suffer need.

I can do all things through Christ which strengtheneth me.

But my God shall supply all your need according to His riches in glory by Christ Jesus.   *Philippians 4:12,13,19*

If What You Hold
    In Your Hand
Is Not Enough
    To Be Your Harvest,
Make It Your Seed.

-MIKE MURDOCK

~ 70 ~

WHEN YOU FACE AN UNEXPECTED FINANCIAL EMERGENCY

And the Lord appeared unto him the same night, and said, I am the God of Abraham thy father: fear not, for I am with thee, and will bless thee, and multiply thy seed for My servant Abraham's sake.   *Genesis 26:24*

Behold, the Lord thy God hath set the land before thee: go up and possess it, as the Lord God of thy fathers hath said unto thee; fear not, neither be discouraged.   *Deuteronomy 1:21*

And shall say unto them, Hear, O Israel, ye approach this day unto battle against your enemies: let not your hearts faint, fear not, and do not tremble, neither be ye terrified because of them;

For the Lord your God is He that goeth with you, to fight for you against your enemies, to save you.

Deuteronomy 20:3,4

The Lord is my light and my salvation; whom shall I fear? the Lord is the strength of my life; of whom shall I be afraid?

Though an host should encamp against me, my heart shall not fear: though war should rise against me, in this will I be confident.   *Psalm 27:1,3*

The angel of the Lord encampeth round about them that fear Him, and delivereth them.

Many are the afflictions of the righteous: but the Lord delivereth him out of them all.   *Psalm 34:7,19*

In God I will praise His word, in God I have put my trust; I will not fear what flesh can do unto me.

Psalm 56:4

The Lord is on my side; I will not fear: what can man do unto me?

It is better to trust in the Lord than to put confidence in man.

Psalm 118:6,8

Strengthen ye the weak hands, and confirm the feeble knees.

Say to them that are of a fearful heart, Be strong, fear not: behold, your God will come with vengeance, even God with a recompence; He will come and save you. *Isaiah 35:3,4*

Fear thou not; for I am with thee: be not dismayed; for I am thy God: I will strengthen thee; yea, I will help thee; yea, I will uphold thee with the right hand of My righteousness.

Isaiah 41:10

Take therefore no thought for the morrow: for the morrow shall take thought for the things of itself. Sufficient unto the day is the evil thereof. *Matthew 6:34*

Not that we are sufficient of ourselves to think any thing as of ourselves; but our sufficiency is of God;

2 Corinthians 3:5

And God is able to make all grace abound toward you; that ye, always having all sufficiency in all things, may abound to every good work:

2 Corinthians 9:8

And He said unto me, My grace is sufficient for thee: for my strength is made perfect in weakness. Most gladly therefore will I rather glory in my infirmities, that the power of Christ may rest upon me. *2 Corinthians 12:9*

Be careful for nothing; but in every thing by prayer and supplication with thanksgiving let your requests be made known unto God.

Not that I speak in respect of want: for I have learned, in whatsoever state I am, therewith to be content.

Philippians 4:6,11

Crisis Always Occurs
At
The Curve Of Change.

-MIKE MURDOCK

❧ 71 ❧

WHEN YOU HAVE SPENT UNWISELY

The steps of a good man are ordered by the Lord: and He delighteth in his way.

Though he fall, he shall not be utterly cast down: for the Lord upholdeth him with His hand.

I have been young, and now am old; yet have I not seen the righteous forsaken, nor his seed begging bread.

Psalm 37:23-25

He will regard the prayer of the destitute, and not despise their prayer.

Psalm 102:17

Remove far from me vanity and lies: give me neither poverty nor riches; feed me with food convenient for me:

Lest I be full, and deny Thee, and say, Who is the Lord? or lest I be poor, and steal, and take the name of my God in vain. *Proverbs 30:8,9*

Fear thou not; for I am with thee: be not dismayed; for I am thy God: I will strengthen thee; yea, I will help thee; yea, I will uphold thee with the right hand of My righteousness.

For I the Lord thy God will hold thy right hand, saying unto thee, Fear not; I will help thee.

Fear not, thou worm Jacob, and ye men of Israel; I will help thee, saith the Lord, and thy redeemer, the Holy One of Israel.

When the poor and needy seek water, and there is none, and their tongue faileth for thirst, I the Lord will hear them, I the God of Israel will not forsake them. *Isaiah 41:10,13,14,17*

Although the fig tree shall not blossom, neither shall fruit be in the vines; the labour of the olive shall fail, and the fields shall yield no meat; the flock shall be cut off from the fold, and there shall be no herd in the stalls:

Yet I will rejoice in the Lord, I will joy in the God of my salvation.

Habakkuk 3:17,18

Therefore I say unto you, Take no thought for your life, what ye shall eat, or what ye shall drink; nor yet for your body, what ye shall put on. Is not the life more than meat, and the body than raiment?

Wherefore, if God so clothe the grass of the field, which to day is, and to morrow is cast into the oven, shall He not much more clothe you, O ye of little faith?

But seek ye first the kingdom of God, and His righteousness; and all these things shall be added unto you.

Take therefore no thought for the morrow: for the morrow shall take thought for the things of itself. Sufficient unto the day is the evil thereof. *Matthew 6:25,30,33,34*

Blessed are ye that hunger now: for ye shall be filled. Blessed are ye that weep now: for ye shall laugh.

Luke 6:21

And we know that all things work together for good to them that love God, to them who are the called according to His purpose.

For I am persuaded, that neither death, nor life, nor angels, nor principalities, nor powers, nor things present, nor things to come,

Nor height, nor depth, nor any other creature, shall be able to separate us from the love of God, which is in Christ Jesus our Lord.

Romans 8:28,38,39

Be careful for nothing; but in every thing by prayer and supplication with thanksgiving let your requests be made known unto God.

And the peace of God, which passeth all understanding, shall keep your hearts and minds through Christ Jesus.

Not that I speak in respect of want: for I have learned, in whatsoever state I am, therewith to be content.

Philippians 4:6,7,11

72

WHEN OTHERS RESENT YOUR SUCCESS

While the earth remaineth, seedtime and harvest, and cold and heat, and summer and winter, and day and night shall not cease. *Genesis 8:22*

The Lord killeth, and maketh alive: He bringeth down to the grave, and bringeth up.

The Lord maketh poor, and maketh rich: He bringeth low, and lifteth up.

He raiseth up the poor out of the dust, and lifteth up the beggar from the dunghill, to set them among princes, and to make them inherit the throne of glory: for the pillars of the earth are the Lord's, and He hath set the world upon them.

He will keep the feet of His saints,

and the wicked shall be silent in darkness; for by strength shall no man prevail.

The adversaries of the Lord shall be broken to pieces; out of heaven shall He thunder upon them: the Lord shall judge the ends of the earth; and He shall give strength unto His king, and exalt the horn of His anointed.

1 Samuel 2:6-10

O that ye would altogether hold your peace! and it should be your wisdom. *Job 13:5*

For there is hope of a tree, if it be cut down, that it will sprout again, and that the tender branch thereof will not cease.

Though the root thereof wax old in the earth, and the stock thereof die in the ground;

Yet through the scent of water it will bud, and bring forth boughs like a plant. *Job 14:7-9*

For the needy shall not alway be forgotten: the expectation of the poor shall not perish for ever.   *Psalm 9:18*

But I will hope continually, and will yet praise Thee more and more.
Psalm 71:14

I will meditate also of all Thy work, and talk of Thy doings.
Psalm 77:12

Trust in the Lord with all thine heart; and lean not unto thine own understanding.

In all thy ways acknowledge Him, and He shall direct thy paths.
Proverbs 3:5,6

If any of you lack wisdom, let him ask of God, that giveth to all men liberally, and upbraideth not; and it shall be given him.   *James 1:5*

But the wisdom that is from above is first pure, then peaceable, gentle, and easy to be intreated, full of mercy and good fruits, without partiality, and without hypocrisy.   *James 3:17*

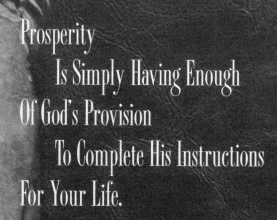

Prosperity
    Is Simply Having Enough
Of God's Provision
        To Complete His Instructions
For Your Life.

-MIKE MURDOCK

∼ 73 ∼

WHEN YOU UNDERTAKE A NEW BUILDING PROGRAM

And they rose early in the morning, and went forth into the wilderness of Tekoa: and as they went forth, Jehoshaphat stood and said, Hear me, O Judah, and ye inhabitants of Jerusalem; Believe in the Lord your God, so shall ye be established; believe His prophets, so shall ye prosper.

2 Chronicles 20:20

Lead me in Thy truth, and teach me: for Thou art the God of my salvation; on Thee do I wait all the day.

Psalm 25:5

Teach me Thy way, O Lord, and lead me in a plain path, because of mine enemies. *Psalm 27:11*

For Thou art my rock and my fortress; therefore for Thy name's sake lead me, and guide me.   *Psalm 31:3*

And I will bring the blind by a way that they knew not; I will lead them in paths that they have not known: I will make darkness light before them, and crooked things straight. These things will I do unto them, and not forsake them.   *Isaiah 42:16*

And the Lord shall guide thee continually, and satisfy thy soul in drought, and make fat thy bones: and thou shalt be like a watered garden, and like a spring of water, whose waters fail not.   *Isaiah 58:11*

Although the fig tree shall not blossom, neither shall fruit be in the vines; the labour of the olive shall fail, and the fields shall yield no meat; the flock shall be cut off from the fold, and there shall be no herd in the stalls:
Yet I will rejoice in the Lord, I will joy in the God of my salvation.
Habakkuk 3:17,18

He is like a man which built an house, and digged deep, and laid the foundation on a rock: and when the flood arose, the stream beat vehemently upon that house, and could not shake it: for it was founded upon a rock.

Luke 6:48

For which of you, intending to build a tower, sitteth not down first, and counteth the cost, whether he have sufficient to finish it?

Lest haply, after he hath laid the foundation, and is not able to finish it, all that behold it begin to mock him,

Saying, This man began to build, and was not able to finish.

Luke 14:28-30

The elder unto the wellbeloved Gaius, whom I love in the truth.

Beloved, I wish above all things that thou mayest prosper and be in health, even as thy soul prospereth.

3 John 1:1,2

⮞ 74 ⮜

WHEN YOU NEED CREATIVE IDEAS FOR RAISING YOUR SUPPORT

⮞▪◦▪⬤

And blessed be the most high God, which hath delivered thine enemies into thy hand. And he gave Him tithes of all. *Genesis 14:20*

And this stone, which I have set for a pillar, shall be God's house: and of all that Thou shalt give me I will surely give the tenth unto Thee.

Genesis 28:22

Speak unto the children of Israel, that they bring Me an offering: of every man that giveth it willingly with his heart ye shall take My offering.

Exodus 25:2

And all the tithe of the land, whether of the seed of the land, or of the fruit of the tree, is the Lord's: it is holy unto the Lord.   *Leviticus 27:30*

Every man shall give as he is able, according to the blessing of the Lord thy God which He hath given thee.
                        Deuteronomy 16:17

The gold for things of gold, and the silver for things of silver, and for all manner of work to be made by the hands of artificers. And who then is willing to consecrate his service this day unto the Lord?

Then the people rejoiced, for that they offered willingly, because with perfect heart they offered willingly to the Lord: and David the king also rejoiced with great joy.
                        1 Chronicles 29:5,9

And as soon as the commandment came abroad, the children of Israel brought in abundance the firstfruits of corn, wine, and oil, and honey, and of all

the increase of the field; and the tithe of all things brought they in abundantly.
2 Chronicles 31:5

Honour the Lord with thy substance, and with the firstfruits of all thine increase: *Proverbs 3:9*

But when thou doest alms, let not thy left hand know what thy right hand doeth: *Matthew 6:3*

Woe unto you, scribes and Pharisees, hypocrites! for ye pay tithe of mint and anise and cummin, and have omitted the weightier matters of the law, judgment, mercy, and faith: these ought ye to have done, and not to leave the other undone. *Matthew 23:23*

Give, and it shall be given unto you; good measure, pressed down, and shaken together, and running over, shall men give into your bosom. For with the same measure that ye mete withal it shall be measured to you again. *Luke 6:38*

Sell that ye have, and give alms; provide yourselves bags which wax not old, a treasure in the heavens that faileth not, where no thief approacheth, neither moth corrupteth.

For where your treasure is, there will your heart be also.   *Luke 12:33,34*

Then the disciples, every man according to his ability, determined to send relief unto the brethren which dwelt in Judaea: *Acts 11:29*

Or he that exhorteth, on exhortation: he that giveth, let him do it with simplicity; he that ruleth, with diligence; he that sheweth mercy, with cheerfulness.   *Romans 12:8*

Moreover it is required in stewards, that a man be found faithful.   *1 Corinthians 4:2*

Upon the first day of the week let every one of you lay by him in store, as God hath prospered him, that there be

no gatherings when I come.
1 Corinthians 16:2

For if there be first a willing mind, it is accepted according to that a man hath, and not according to that he hath not. *2 Corinthians 8:12*

But this I say, He which soweth sparingly shall reap also sparingly; and he which soweth bountifully shall reap also bountifully.

Every man according as he purposeth in his heart, so let him give; not grudgingly, or of necessity: for God loveth a cheerful giver.
2 Corinthians 9:6,7

Be not deceived; God is not mocked: for whatsoever a man soweth, that shall he also reap. *Galatians 6:7*

As every man hath received the gift, even so minister the same one to another, as good stewards of the manifold grace of God. *1 Peter 4:10*

❧ 75 ❧

WHEN YOU NEED A FINANCIAL MIRACLE

Thou shalt make thy prayer unto Him, and He shall hear thee, and thou shalt pay thy vows.   *Job 22:27*

I will call upon the Lord, Who is worthy to be praised: so shall I be saved from mine enemies.   *Psalm 18:3*

The eyes of the Lord are upon the righteous, and His ears are open unto their cry.   *Psalm 34:15*

But thou, when thou prayest, enter into thy closet, and when thou hast shut thy door, pray to thy Father which is in secret; and thy Father which seeth in secret shall reward thee openly.

Give us this day our daily bread.

Therefore I say unto you, Take no

thought for your life, what ye shall eat, or what ye shall drink; nor yet for your body, what ye shall put on. Is not the life more than meat, and the body than raiment? *Matthew 6:6,11,25*

Ask, and it shall be given you; seek, and ye shall find; knock, and it shall be opened unto you:

For every one that asketh receiveth; and he that seeketh findeth; and to him that knocketh it shall be opened. *Matthew 7:7,8*

Again I say unto you, That if two of you shall agree on earth as touching any thing that they shall ask, it shall be done for them of my Father which is in heaven. *Matthew 18:19*

But Jesus beheld them, and said unto them, With men this is impossible; but with God all things are possible. *Matthew 19:26*

And all things, whatsoever ye shall ask in prayer, believing, ye shall receive. *Matthew 21:22*

YOUR PERSONAL MOTIVATION AND ADVERSITY

⮾ 76 ⮾

WHEN YOU FACE "BURN-OUT"

━━━━◆━━━━

For there is hope of a tree, if it be cut down, that it will sprout again, and that the tender branch thereof will not cease.   *Job 14:7*

I have set the Lord always before me: because He is at my right hand, I shall not be moved.

Therefore my heart is glad, and my glory rejoiceth: my flesh also shall rest in hope.   *Psalm 16:8,9*

He restoreth my soul: He leadeth me in the paths of righteousness for His name's sake. *Psalm 23:3*

For in Thee, O Lord, do I hope: Thou wilt hear, O Lord my God.
Psalm 38:15

Why art thou cast down, O my soul? and why art thou disquieted in me? hope thou in God: for I shall yet praise Him for the help of His countenance. *Psalm 42:5*

Create in me a clean heart, O God; and renew a right spirit within me.
Psalm 51:10

But I will hope continually, and will yet praise Thee more and more.
Psalm 71:14

The righteous shall flourish like the palm tree: he shall grow like a cedar in Lebanon. *Psalm 92:12*

Those that be planted in the house

of the Lord shall flourish in the courts of our God.

They shall still bring forth fruit in old age; they shall be fat and flourishing; *Psalm 92:13,14*

Who redeemeth thy life from destruction; Who crowneth thee with lovingkindness and tender mercies;

Who satisfieth thy mouth with good things; so that thy youth is renewed like the eagle's. *Psalm 103:4,5*

I wait for the Lord, my soul doth wait, and in His word do I hope.

My soul waiteth for the Lord more than they that watch for the morning: I say, more than they that watch for the morning. *Psalm 130:5,6*

But they that wait upon the Lord shall renew their strength; they shall mount up with wings as eagles; they shall run, and not be weary; and they shall walk, and not faint. *Isaiah 40:31*

For I will pour water upon him

that is thirsty, and floods upon the dry ground: I will pour My spirit upon thy seed, and My blessing upon thine offspring: *Isaiah 44:3*

Turn thou us unto Thee, O Lord, and we shall be turned; renew our days as of old.   *Lamentations 5:21*

And all the trees of the field shall know that I the Lord have brought down the high tree, have exalted the low tree, have dried up the green tree, and have made the dry tree to flourish: I the Lord have spoken and have done it.   *Ezekiel 17:24*

Again He said unto me, Prophesy upon these bones, and say unto them, O ye dry bones, hear the word of the Lord.

Thus saith the Lord God unto these bones; Behold, I will cause breath to enter into you, and ye shall live:

And I will lay sinews upon you, and will bring up flesh upon you, and cover you with skin, and put breath in you, and ye shall live; and ye shall know that I am the Lord.   *Ezekiel 37:4-6*

And I will restore to you the years that the locust hath eaten, the cankerworm, and the caterpiller, and the palmerworm, My great army which I sent among you.   *Joel 2:25*

I am the vine, ye are the branches: He that abideth in Me, and I in him, the same bringeth forth much fruit: for without Me ye can do nothing.

Herein is my Father glorified, that ye bear much fruit; so shall ye be My disciples.   *John 15:5,8*

And be not conformed to this world: but be ye transformed by the renewing of your mind, that ye may prove what is that good, and acceptable, and perfect, will of God.

Rejoicing in hope; patient in tribulation; continuing instant in prayer;   *Romans 12:2,12*

For which cause we faint not; but though our outward man perish, yet the inward man is renewed day by day.

While we look not at the things which are seen, but at the things which are not seen: for the things which are seen are temporal; but the things which are not seen are eternal.

2 Corinthians 4:16,18

Now a mediator is not a mediator of one, but God is one.   *Galatians 3:20*

And be renewed in the spirit of your mind;   *Ephesians 4:23*

Brethren, I count not myself to have apprehended: but this one thing I do, forgetting those things which are behind, and reaching forth unto those things which are before,

I press toward the mark for the prize of the high calling of God in Christ Jesus.   *Philippians 3:13,14*

I can do all things through Christ which strengtheneth me.

Philippians 4:13

❧ 77 ❧

WHEN YOU DO NOT FEEL INSPIRED TO MINISTER

And they said, Arise, that we may go up against them: for we have seen the land, and, behold, it is very good: and are ye still? be not slothful to go, and to enter to possess the land.

Judges 18:9

And David was greatly distressed; for the people spake of stoning him, because the soul of all the people was grieved, every man for his sons and for his daughters: but David encouraged himself in the Lord his God.

1 Samuel 30:6

For the ear trieth words, as the mouth tasteth meat.

Let us choose to us judgment: let

us know among ourselves what is good.
Job 34:3,4

A good man sheweth favour, and lendeth: he will guide his affairs with discretion. *Psalm 112:5*

He that gathereth in summer is a wise son: but he that sleepeth in harvest is a son that causeth shame.
Proverbs 10:5

The hand of the diligent shall bear rule: but the slothful shall be under tribute. *Proverbs 12:24*

I went by the field of the slothful, and by the vineyard of the man void of understanding;

And, lo, it was all grown over with thorns, and nettles had covered the face thereof, and the stone wall thereof was broken down.

Then I saw, and considered it well: I looked upon it, and received instruction.

Yet a little sleep, a little slumber, a little folding of the hands to sleep:

So shall thy poverty come as one that travelleth; and thy want as an armed man.   *Proverbs 24:30-34*

As the door turneth upon his hinges, so doth the slothful upon his bed.   *Proverbs 26:14*

By much slothfulness the building decayeth; and through idleness of the hands the house droppeth through.
Ecclesiastes 10:18

Who is wise, and he shall understand these things? prudent, and he shall know them? for the ways of the Lord are right, and the just shall walk in them: but the transgressors shall fall therein.   *Hosea 14:9*

Ask, and it shall be given you; seek, and ye shall find; knock, and it shall be opened unto you:
For every one that asketh receiveth; and he that seeketh findeth; and to him that knocketh it shall be opened.   *Matthew 7:7,8*

Bless them which persecute you: bless, and curse not.   *Romans 12:14*

And He said unto me, My grace is sufficient for thee: for My strength is made perfect in weakness. Most gladly therefore will I rather glory in my infirmities, that the power of Christ may rest upon me. *2 Corinthians 12:9*

Wherefore he saith, Awake thou that sleepest, and arise from the dead, and Christ shall give thee light.
Ephesians 5:14

Walk in wisdom toward them that are without, redeeming the time.
And say to Archippus, Take heed to the ministry which thou hast received in the Lord, that thou fulfill it.
Colossians 4:5,17

Let him eschew evil, and do good; let him seek peace, and ensue it.
For the eyes of the Lord are over the righteous, and his ears are open unto their prayers: but the face of the Lord is against them that do evil.
1 Peter 3:11,12

≈ 78 ≈

WHEN YOU FEEL MISUNDERSTOOD BY THOSE YOU LOVE

Cease from anger, and forsake wrath: fret not thyself in any wise to do evil. *Psalm 37:8*

A soft answer turneth away wrath: but grievous words stir up anger.

The tongue of the wise useth knowledge aright: but the mouth of fools poureth out foolishness.

Proverbs 15:1,2

Go not forth hastily to strive, lest thou know not what to do in the end thereof, when thy neighbour hath put thee to shame. *Proverbs 25:8*

Be not hasty in thy spirit to be angry: for anger resteth in the bosom of fools. *Ecclesiastes 7:9*

Blessed are they that mourn: for they shall be comforted. *Matthew 5:4*

The Spirit of the Lord is upon me, because He hath anointed me to preach the gospel to the poor; He hath sent me to heal the brokenhearted, to preach deliverance to the captives, and recovering of sight to the blind, to set at liberty them that are bruised, *Luke 4:18*

Then said the Lord, Doest thou well to be angry? *John 4:4*

I will not leave you comfortless: I will come to you. *John 14:18*

And be not conformed to this world: but be ye transformed by the renewing of your mind, that ye may prove what is that good, and acceptable, and perfect, will of God.

Dearly beloved, avenge not yourselves, but rather give place unto wrath: for it is written, Vengeance is Mine; I will repay, saith the Lord.
Romans 12:2,19

The Only Reason
Men Fail
Is Broken Focus.

-MIKE MURDOCK

⇜ 79 ⇝

WHEN ADMINISTRATIVE PROBLEMS DISTRACT YOU FROM SPIRITUAL RESPONSIBILITIES

⇒•◦•⇐

And thou, Solomon my son, know thou the God of thy father, and serve Him with a perfect heart and with a willing mind: for the Lord searcheth all hearts, and understandeth all the imaginations of the thoughts: if thou seek Him, He will be found of thee; but if thou forsake Him, He will cast thee off for ever.   *1 Chronicles 28:9*

And he went out to meet Asa, and said unto him, Hear ye me, Asa, and all Judah and Benjamin; The Lord is with you, while ye be with Him; and if ye seek Him, He will be found of you; but if

ye forsake Him, He will forsake you.
2 Chronicles 15:2

But as for me, my feet were almost
gone; my steps had well nigh slipped.

For I was envious at the foolish,
when I saw the prosperity of the
wicked.

When I thought to know this, it
was too painful for me; *Psalm 73:2,3,16*

And the cares of this world, and
the deceitfulness of riches, and the lusts
of other things entering in, choke the
word, and it becometh unfruitful.
Mark 4:19

And that which fell among thorns
are they, which, when they have heard,
go forth, and are choked with cares and
riches and pleasures of this life, and
bring no fruit to perfection. *Luke 8:14*

And take heed to yourselves, lest
at any time your hearts be overcharged
with surfeiting, and drunkenness, and
cares of this life, and so that day come

upon you unawares.   *Luke 21:34*

And God is able to make all grace abound toward you; that ye, always having all sufficiency in all things, may abound to every good work:
2 Corinthians 9:8

Ye did run well; who did hinder you that ye should not obey the truth?
Galatians 5:7

Neglect not the gift that is in thee, which was given thee by prophecy, with the laying on of the hands of the presbytery.   *1 Timothy 4:14*

How shall we escape, if we neglect so great salvation; which at the first began to be spoken by the Lord, and was confirmed unto us by them that heard Him;   *Hebrews 2:3*

Let us draw near with a true heart in full assurance of faith, having our hearts sprinkled from an evil conscience, and our bodies washed with pure water.

Let us hold fast the profession of our faith without wavering; for He is faithful that promised;

And let us consider one another to provoke unto love and to good works:

Not forsaking the assembling of ourselves together, as the manner of some is; but exhorting one another: and so much the more, as ye see the day approaching.   *Hebrews 10:22-25*

Wherefore seeing we also are compassed about with so great a cloud of witnesses, let us lay aside every weight, and the sin which doth so easily beset us, and let us run with patience the race that is set before us,

Looking unto Jesus the author and finisher of our faith; Who for the joy that was set before Him endured the cross, despising the shame, and is set down at the right hand of the throne of God.   *Hebrews 12:1,2*

When You Change
Your Focus
You Will Change
Your Feelings.

-MIKE MURDOCK

❧ 80 ❧

WHEN FINANCIAL WORRIES STEAL YOUR JOY

For Thou art my lamp, O Lord: and the Lord will lighten my darkness.
2 Samuel 22:29

Blessed is the man that walketh not in the counsel of the ungodly, nor standeth in the way of sinners, nor sitteth in the seat of the scornful.

But his delight is in the law of the Lord; and in His law doth he meditate day and night. *Psalm 1:1,2*

Lead me, O Lord, in Thy righteousness because of mine enemies; make Thy way straight before my face.
Psalm 5:8

Thou wilt shew me the path of life: in Thy presence is fulness of joy; at Thy right hand there are pleasures for evermore.   *Psalm 16:11*

The Lord is my shepherd; I shall not want.

He maketh me to lie down in green pastures: He leadeth me beside the still waters.

He restoreth my soul: He leadeth me in the paths of righteousness for His name's sake.   *Psalm 23:1-3*

Lead me in Thy truth, and teach me: for Thou art the God of my salvation; on Thee do I wait all the day.

What man is he that feareth the Lord? him shall He teach in the way that he shall choose.   *Psalm 25:5,12*

The Lord is my light and my salvation; whom shall I fear? the Lord is the strength of my life; of whom shall I be afraid?

Teach me Thy way, O Lord, and lead me in a plain path, because of mine enemies.   *Psalm 27:1,11*

For Thou art my rock and my fortress; therefore for Thy name's sake lead me, and guide me.   *Psalm 31:3*

And I will bring the blind by a way that they knew not; I will lead them in paths that they have not known: I will make darkness light before them, and crooked things straight. These things will I do unto them, and not forsake them.   *Isaiah 42:16*

And the Lord shall guide thee continually, and satisfy thy soul in drought, and make fat thy bones: and thou shalt be like a watered garden, and like a spring of water, whose waters fail not.   *Isaiah 58:11*

Call unto Me, and I will answer thee, and shew thee great and mighty things, which thou knowest not.
                    Jeremiah 33:3

You Are Never As Far
From A Miracle
As It First Appears.

-MIKE MURDOCK

～ 81 ～

WHEN YOU ARE INEXPERIENCED IN MINISTRY

And Caleb stilled the people before Moses, and said, Let us go up at once, and possess it; for we are well able to overcome it.   *Numbers 13:30*

Give therefore Thy servant an understanding heart to judge Thy people, that I may discern between good and bad: for who is able to judge this Thy so great a people?   *1 Kings 3:9*

Be ye strong therefore, and let not your hands be weak: for your work shall be rewarded.   *2 Chronicles 15:7*

Have mercy upon me, O Lord; for I

am weak: O Lord, heal me; for my
bones are vexed. *Psalm 6:2*

Wait on the Lord: be of good
courage, and He shall strengthen thine
heart: wait, I say, on the Lord.
Psalm 27:14

Be of good courage, and He shall
strengthen your heart, all ye that hope
in the Lord. *Psalm 31:24*

Wisdom is the principal thing;
therefore get wisdom: and with all thy
getting get understanding. *Proverbs 4:7*

Counsel is mine, and sound
wisdom: I am understanding; I have
strength. *Proverbs 8:14*

And by knowledge shall the
chambers be filled with all precious and
pleasant riches.
A wise man is strong; yea, a man of
knowledge increaseth strength.
For by wise counsel thou shalt
make thy war: and in multitude of

counsellors there is safety.

Proverbs 24:4-6

Wisdom strengtheneth the wise more than ten mighty men which are in the city. *Ecclesiastes 7:19*

If the iron be blunt, and he do not whet the edge, then must he put to more strength: but wisdom is profitable to direct. *Ecclesiastes 10:10*

Strengthen ye the weak hands, and confirm the feeble knees.

Say to them that are of a fearful heart, Be strong, fear not: behold, your God will come with vengeance, even God with a recompence; He will come and save you. *Isaiah 35:3,4*

Fear thou not; for I am with thee: be not dismayed; for I am thy God: I will strengthen thee; yea, I will help thee; yea, I will uphold thee with the right hand of My righteousness.

Isaiah 41:10

Who against hope believed in hope, that he might become the father of many nations, according to that which was spoken, So shall thy seed be.

And being not weak in faith, he considered not his own body now dead, when he was about an hundred years old, neither yet the deadness of Sarah's womb:

He staggered not at the promise of God through unbelief; but was strong in faith, giving glory to God;

And being fully persuaded that, what He had promised, He was able also to perform.   *Romans 4:18-21*

But God hath chosen the foolish things of the world to confound the wise; and God hath chosen the weak things of the world to confound the things which are mighty;

1 Corinthians 1:27

For to one is given by the Spirit the word of wisdom; to another the word of knowledge by the same Spirit;

1 Corinthians 12:8

And God is able to make all grace abound toward you; that ye, always having all sufficiency in all things, may abound to every good work:
2 Corinthians 9:8

And He said unto me, My grace is sufficient for thee: for My strength is made perfect in weakness. Most gladly therefore will I rather glory in my infirmities, that the power of Christ may rest upon me.

Therefore I take pleasure in infirmities, in reproaches, in necessities, in persecutions, in distresses for Christ's sake: for when I am weak, then am I strong. *2 Corinthians 12:9,10*

That He would grant you, according to the riches of His glory, to be strengthened with might by His Spirit in the inner man;

Now unto Him that is able to do exceeding abundantly above all that we ask or think, according to the power that worketh in us, *Ephesians 3:16,20*

I can do all things through Christ which strengtheneth me.

Philippians 4:13

I thank God, Whom I serve from my forefathers with pure conscience, that without ceasing I have remembrance of thee in my prayers night and day;

Greatly desiring to see thee, being mindful of thy tears, that I may be filled with joy;

When I call to remembrance the unfeigned faith that is in Thee, which dwelt first in thy grandmother Lois, and thy mother Eunice; and I am persuaded that in Thee also.

Wherefore I put Thee in remembrance that Thou stir up the gift of God, which is in Thee by the putting on of my hands. *2 Timothy 1:3-6*

Thou therefore, my son, be strong in the grace that is in Christ Jesus.

And the things that thou hast heard of me among many witnesses, the same commit thou to faithful men, who

shall be able to teach others also.
                    2 Timothy 2:1,2

Through faith also Sara herself received strength to conceive seed, and was delivered of a child when she was past age, because she judged Him faithful Who had promised.
Quenched the violence of fire, escaped the edge of the sword, out of weakness were made strong, waxed valiant in fight, turned to flight the armies of the aliens. *Hebrews 11:11,34*

If any of you lack wisdom, let him ask of God, that giveth to all men liberally, and upbraideth not; and it shall be given him.   *James 1:5*

～ 82 ～

WHEN YOU FEEL LONELY AND UNAPPRECIATED

Yea, though I walk through the valley of the shadow of death, I will fear no evil: for Thou art with me; Thy rod and Thy staff they comfort me.

Psalm 23:4

I was a reproach among all mine enemies, but especially among my neighbours, and a fear to mine acquaintance: they that did see me without fled from me.

I am forgotten as a dead man out of mind: I am like a broken vessel.

My times are in Thy hand: deliver me from the hand of mine enemies, and from them that persecute me.

Psalm 31:11,12,15

I have been young, and now am

old; yet have I not seen the righteous forsaken, nor his seed begging bread.

For the Lord loveth judgment, and forsaketh not His saints; they are preserved for ever: but the seed of the wicked shall be cut off. *Psalm 37:25,28*

Save me, O God; for the waters are come in unto my soul.

I sink in deep mire, where there is no standing: I am come into deep waters, where the floods overflow me.

I am weary of my crying: my throat is dried: mine eyes fail while I wait for my God. *Psalm 69:1-3*

In the day of my trouble I sought the Lord: my sore ran in the night, and ceased not: my soul refused to be comforted. *Psalm 77:2*

He healeth the broken in heart, and bindeth up their wounds.

Psalm 147:3

A man that hath friends must shew himself friendly: and there is a friend that sticketh closer than a brother. *Proverbs 18:24*

For Thou hast been a strength to the poor, a strength to the needy in his distress, a refuge from the storm, a shadow from the heat, when the blast of the terrible ones is as a storm against the wall. *Isaiah 25:4*

He giveth power to the faint; and to them that have no might He increaseth strength. *Isaiah 40:29*

Fear Thou not; for I am with thee: be not dismayed; for I am thy God: I will strengthen thee; yea, I will help thee; yea, I will uphold thee with the right hand of My righteousness.

For I the Lord thy God will hold thy right hand, saying unto thee, Fear not; I will help thee. *Isaiah 41:10,13*

Are not two sparrows sold for a farthing? and one of them shall not fall on the ground without your Father.

But the very hairs of your head are all numbered.

Fear ye not therefore, ye are of more value than many sparrows.

Matthew 10:29-31

And I will pray the Father, and He shall give you another Comforter, that He may abide with you for ever;

Even the Spirit of truth; Whom the world cannot receive, because it seeth Him not, neither knoweth Him: but ye know Him; for He dwelleth with you, and shall be in you.

I will not leave you comfortless: I will come to you.

Peace I leave with you, My peace I give unto you: not as the world giveth, give I unto you. Let not your heart be troubled, neither let it be afraid.

John 14:16-18,27

Blessed be God, even the Father of our Lord Jesus Christ, the Father of mercies, and the God of all comfort;

Who comforteth us in all our tribulation, that we may be able to comfort them which are in any trouble, by the comfort wherewith we ourselves are comforted of God.

2 Corinthians 1:3,4

Nevertheless God, that comforteth those that are cast down, comforted us by the coming of Titus;

2 Corinthians 7:6

At my first answer no man stood with me, but all men forsook me: I pray God that it may not be laid to their charge.

Notwithstanding the Lord stood with me, and strengthened me; that by me the preaching might be fully known, and that all the Gentiles might hear: and I was delivered out of the mouth of the lion.

And the Lord shall deliver me from every evil work, and will preserve me unto His heavenly kingdom: to Whom be glory for ever and ever. Amen.

2 Timothy 4:16-18

For we have not an high priest which cannot be touched with the feeling of our infirmities; but was in all points tempted like as we are, yet without sin.

Let us therefore come boldly unto the throne of grace, that we may obtain mercy, and find grace to help in time of need. *Hebrews 4:15,16*

Let your conversation be without covetousness; and be content with such things as ye have: for He hath said, I will never leave thee, nor forsake thee.
Hebrews 13:5

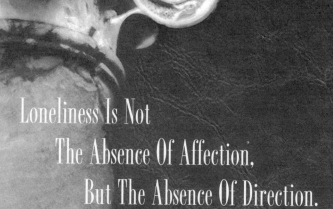

Loneliness Is Not
The Absence Of Affection,
But The Absence Of Direction.

-MIKE MURDOCK

∾ 83 ∾

WHEN YOUR VISION FOR THE MINISTRY FADES

And the Lord, He it is that doth go before thee; He will be with thee, He will not fail thee, neither forsake thee: fear not, neither be dismayed.

Deuteronomy 31:8

Have not I commanded thee? Be strong and of a good courage; be not afraid, neither be thou dismayed: for the Lord thy God is with thee whithersoever thou goest.   *Joshua 1:9*

Be ye strong therefore, and let not your hands be weak: for your work shall be rewarded.   *2 Chronicles 15:7*

For the eyes of the Lord run to and fro throughout the whole earth, to shew

Himself strong in the behalf of them whose heart is perfect toward Him. Herein thou hast done foolishly: therefore from henceforth thou shalt have wars.   *2 Chronicles 16:9*

And they rose early in the morning, and went forth into the wilderness of Tekoa: and as they went forth, Jehoshaphat stood and said, Hear me, O Judah, and ye inhabitants of Jerusalem; Believe in the Lord your God, so shall ye be established; believe His prophets, so shall ye prosper.
                    2 Chronicles 20:20

Offer the sacrifices of righteousness, and put your trust in the Lord.
                    Psalm 4:5

Wait on the Lord: be of good courage, and He shall strengthen thine heart: wait, I say, on the Lord.
                    Psalm 27:14

Trust in the Lord, and do good; so shalt thou dwell in the land, and verily thou shalt be fed.

Commit thy way unto the Lord; trust also in Him; and He shall bring it to pass. *Psalm 37:3,5*

Cast thy burden upon the Lord, and He shall sustain thee: He shall never suffer the righteous to be moved. *Psalm 55:22*

Trust in the Lord with all thine heart; and lean not unto thine own understanding.

In all thy ways acknowledge Him, and He shall direct thy paths.

Be not afraid of sudden fear, neither of the desolation of the wicked, when it cometh.

For the Lord shall be thy confidence, and shall keep thy foot from being taken. *Proverbs 3:5,6,25,26*

Righteous lips are the delight of kings; and they love him that speaketh right. *Proverbs 16:13*

Thou wilt keep him in perfect

peace, whose mind is stayed on Thee: because he trusteth in Thee. *Isaiah 26:3*

Fear thou not; for I am with thee: be not dismayed; for I am thy God: I will strengthen thee; yea, I will help thee; yea, I will uphold thee with the right hand of My righteousness. *Isaiah 41:10*

I have declared, and have saved, and I have shewed, when there was no strange god among you: therefore ye are My witnesses, saith the Lord, that I am God. *Isaiah 43:12*

Although the fig tree shall not blossom, neither shall fruit be in the vines; the labour of the olive shall fail, and the fields shall yield no meat; the flock shall be cut off from the fold, and there shall be no herd in the stalls:

Yet I will rejoice in the Lord, I will joy in the God of my salvation.

The Lord God is my strength, and He will make my feet like hinds' feet, and He will make me to walk upon mine high places. To the chief singer on

my stringed instruments.
Habakkuk 3:17-19

The Lord thy God in the midst of thee is mighty; He will save, He will rejoice over thee with joy; He will rest in His love, He will joy over thee with singing. *Zephaniah 3:17*

Wherefore, if God so clothe the grass of the field, which to day is, and to morrow is cast into the oven, shall He not much more clothe you, O ye of little faith? *Matthew 6:30*

And Jesus said unto them, Because of your unbelief: for verily I say unto you, If ye have faith as a grain of mustard seed, ye shall say unto this mountain, Remove hence to yonder place; and it shall remove; and nothing shall be impossible unto you.
Matthew 17:20

And the Lord said, If ye had faith as a grain of mustard seed, ye might say unto this sycamine tree, Be thou plucked up by the root, and be thou planted in the sea; and it should obey you. *Luke 17:6*

That He would grant you, according to the riches of His glory, to be strengthened with might by His Spirit in the inner man;

That Christ may dwell in your hearts by faith; that ye, being rooted and grounded in love,

May be able to comprehend with all saints what is the breadth, and length, and depth, and height;

And to know the love of Christ, which passeth knowledge, that ye might be filled with all the fulness of God. *Ephesians 3:16-19*

∾ 84 ∾

WHEN YOU FIND IT DIFFICULT TO SLEEP

I will both lay me down in peace, and sleep: for Thou, Lord, only makest me dwell in safety.   *Psalm 4:8*

Fret not thyself because of evildoers, neither be thou envious against the workers of iniquity.

Commit thy way unto the Lord; trust also in Him; and He shall bring it to pass.

Rest in the Lord, and wait patiently for him: fret not thyself because of him who prospereth in his way, because of the man who bringeth wicked devices to pass.

Cease from anger, and forsake wrath: fret not thyself in any wise to do evil.

But the meek shall inherit the earth; and shall delight themselves in the abundance of peace.

Psalm 37:1,5,7,8,11

Cast thy burden upon the Lord, and He shall sustain thee: He shall never suffer the righteous to be moved.

Psalm 55:22

It is vain for you to rise up early, to sit up late, to eat the bread of sorrows: for so He giveth His beloved sleep.

Psalm 127:2

When thou liest down, thou shalt not be afraid: yea, thou shalt lie down, and thy sleep shall be sweet.

Proverbs 3:24

My son, keep thy father's commandment, and forsake not the law of thy mother:

Bind them continually upon thine heart, and tie them about thy neck.

When thou goest, it shall lead thee;

when thou sleepest, it shall keep thee; and when thou awakest, it shall talk with thee. *Proverbs 6:20-22*

Fret not thyself because of evil men, neither be thou envious at the wicked; *Proverbs 24:19*

Thou wilt keep him in perfect peace, whose mind is stayed on Thee: because he trusteth in Thee.

Isaiah 26:3

And My people shall dwell in a peaceable habitation, and in sure dwellings, and in quiet resting places;

Isaiah 32:18

Blessed is the man that trusteth in the Lord, and whose hope the Lord is.

For he shall be as a tree planted by the waters, and that spreadeth out her roots by the river, and shall not see when heat cometh, but her leaf shall be green; and shall not be careful in the year of drought, neither shall cease from yielding fruit. *Jeremiah 17:7,8*

Therefore I say unto you, Take no thought for your life, what ye shall eat, or what ye shall drink; nor yet for your body, what ye shall put on. Is not the life more than meat, and the body than raiment?

But seek ye first the kingdom of God, and His righteousness; and all these things shall be added unto you.

Take therefore no thought for the morrow: for the morrow shall take thought for the things of itself. Sufficient unto the day is the evil thereof.   *Matthew 6:25,33,34*

And take heed to yourselves, lest at any time your hearts be overcharged with surfeiting, and drunkenness, and cares of this life, and so that day come upon you unawares.   *Luke 21:34*

Peter therefore was kept in prison: but prayer was made without ceasing of the church unto God for him.

And when Herod would have brought him forth, the same night Peter was sleeping between two soldiers, bound with two chains: and the keepers before the door kept the prison.

Acts 12:5,6

For to be carnally minded is death; but to be spiritually minded is life and peace. *Romans 8:6*

Be careful for nothing; but in every thing by prayer and supplication with thanksgiving let your requests be made known unto God.

And the peace of God, which passeth all understanding, shall keep your hearts and minds through Christ Jesus. *Philippians 4:6,7*

No man that warreth entangleth himself with the affairs of this life; that he may please Him who hath chosen him to be a soldier. *2 Timothy 2:4*

Let your conversation be without covetousness; and be content with such things as ye have: for He hath said, I will never leave thee, nor forsake thee.

Hebrews 13:5

When Fatigue
Walks In,
Faith Walks Out.

-MIKE MURDOCK

❧ 85 ❧

WHEN YOU FEEL LIKE QUITTING THE MINISTRY

I had fainted, unless I had believed to see the goodness of the Lord in the land of the living.

Wait on the Lord: be of good courage, and He shall strengthen thine heart: wait, I say, on the Lord.

Psalm 27:13,14

Be of good courage, and He shall strengthen your heart, all ye that hope in the Lord.   *Psalm 31:24*

For in Thee, O Lord, do I hope: Thou wilt hear, O Lord my God.   *Psalm 38:15*

And now, Lord, what wait I for? my hope is in Thee.   *Psalm 39:7*

Why art thou cast down, O my soul? and why art thou disquieted within me? hope in God: for I shall yet praise Him, Who is the health of my countenance, and my God. *Psalm 43:5*

For Thou art my hope, O Lord God: Thou art my trust from my youth.

But I will hope continually, and will yet praise Thee more and more.
Psalm 71:5,14

My soul fainteth for Thy salvation: but I hope in Thy word.

Lord, I have hoped for Thy salvation, and done Thy command-ments. *Psalm 119:81,166*

Happy is he that hath the God of Jacob for his help, whose hope is in the Lord his God: *Psalm 146:5*

Trust in the Lord with all thine heart; and lean not unto thine own understanding. *Proverbs 3:5*

Hope deferred maketh the heart sick: but when the desire cometh, it is a tree of life.   *Proverbs 13:12*

For surely there is an end; and thine expectation shall not be cut off.
                                   Proverbs 23:18

So shall the knowledge of wisdom be unto thy soul: when thou hast found it, then there shall be a reward, and thy expectation shall not be cut off.
                                   Proverbs 24:14

Blessed is the man that trusteth in the Lord, and whose hope the Lord is.
                                   Jeremiah 17:7

The Lord is my portion, saith my soul; therefore will I hope in Him.
It is good that a man should both hope and quietly wait for the salvation of the Lord.   *Lamentations 3:24,26*

Jesus said unto him, If thou canst believe, all things are possible to him that believeth.
And straightway the father of the child cried out, and said with tears,

Lord, I believe; help thou mine unbelief.
Mark 9:23,24

For verily I say unto you, That whosoever shall say unto this mountain, Be thou removed, and be thou cast into the sea; and shall not doubt in his heart, but shall believe that those things which he saith shall come to pass; he shall have whatsoever he saith.

Therefore I say unto you, What things soever ye desire, when ye pray, believe that ye receive them, and ye shall have them. *Mark 11:23,24*

Who against hope believed in hope, that he might become the father of many nations, according to that which was spoken, So shall thy seed be.
Romans 4:18

But if we hope for that we see not, then do we with patience wait for it.
Romans 8:25

Rejoicing in hope; patient in

tribulation; continuing instant in prayer;   *Romans 12:12*

For whatsoever things were written aforetime were written for our learning, that we through patience and comfort of the scriptures might have hope.

Now the God of hope fill you with all joy and peace in believing, that ye may abound in hope, through the power of the Holy Ghost.   *Romans 15:4,13*

And take the helmet of salvation, and the sword of the Spirit, which is the word of God:

Praying always with all prayer and supplication in the Spirit, and watching thereunto with all perseverance and supplication for all saints;

Ephesians 6:17,18

Faithful is He that calleth you, Who also will do it.   *1 Thessalonians 5:24*

～ 86 ～

WHEN YOU FEEL DEPRESSED

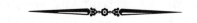

For the needy shall not alway be forgotten: the expectation of the poor shall not perish for ever.   *Psalm 9:18*

Be of good courage, and He shall strengthen your heart, all ye that hope in the Lord.   *Psalm 31:24*

Behold, the eye of the Lord is upon them that fear Him, upon them that hope in His mercy;
To deliver their soul from death, and to keep them alive in famine.
Psalm 33:18,19

For in Thee, O Lord, do I hope: Thou wilt hear, O Lord my God.   *Psalm 38:15*

Why art thou cast down, O my soul? and why art thou disquieted within me? hope in God: for I shall yet praise Him, Who is the health of my countenance, and my God. *Psalm 43:5*

For Thou art my hope, O Lord God: thou art my trust from my youth.

But I will hope continually, and will yet praise Thee more and more.

Psalm 71:5,14

Happy is he that hath the God of Jacob for his help, whose hope is in the Lord his God: *Psalm 146:5*

Hope deferred maketh the heart sick: but when the desire cometh, it is a tree of life. *Proverbs 13:12*

Let not thine heart envy sinners: but be thou in the fear of the Lord all the day long.

For surely there is an end; and thine expectation shall not be cut off.

Proverbs 23:17,18

Who against hope believed in

hope, that he might become the father of many nations, according to that which was spoken, So shall thy seed be.

And being not weak in faith, he considered not his own body now dead, when he was about an hundred years old, neither yet the deadness of Sarah's womb: *Romans 4:18,19*

Rejoicing in hope; patient in tribulation; continuing instant in prayer; *Romans 12:12*

Now the God of hope fill you with all joy and peace in believing, that ye may abound in hope, through the power of the Holy Ghost. *Romans 15:13*

There hath no temptation taken you but such as is common to man: but God is faithful, who will not suffer you to be tempted above that ye are able; but will with the temptation also make a way to escape, that ye may be able to bear it. *1 Corinthians 10:13*

And God is able to make all grace abound toward you; that ye, always having all sufficiency in all things, may abound to every good work:

2 Corinthians 9:8

Finally, brethren, whatsoever things are true, whatsoever things are honest, whatsoever things are just, whatsoever things are pure, whatsoever things are lovely, whatsoever things are of good report; if there be any virtue, and if there be any praise, think on these things. *Philippians 4:8*

Be sober, be vigilant; because your adversary the devil, as a roaring lion, walketh about, seeking whom he may devour:

Whom resist stedfast in the faith, knowing that the same afflictions are accomplished in your brethren that are in the world.

But the God of all grace, Who hath called us unto His eternal glory by Christ Jesus, after that ye have suffered a while, make you perfect, stablish, strengthen, settle you.

1 Peter 5:8-10

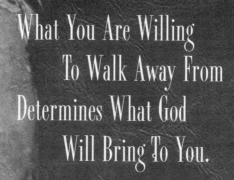

What You Are Willing
To Walk Away From
Determines What God
Will Bring To You.

-MIKE MURDOCK

～ 87 ～

WHEN YOU FACE SEXUAL TEMPTATIONS

And it came to pass after these things, that his master's wife cast her eyes upon Joseph; and she said, Lie with me.

But he refused, and said unto his master's wife, Behold, my master wotteth not what is with me in the house, and he hath committed all that he hath to my hand;

And it came to pass, as she spake to Joseph day by day, that he hearkened not unto her, to lie by her, or to be with her.

And it came to pass about this time, that Joseph went into the house to do his business; and there was none of the men of the house there within.

Genesis 39:7,8,10,11

But he knoweth not that the dead are there; and that her guests are in the depths of hell.   *Proverbs 9:18*

Ye have heard that it was said by them of old time, Thou shalt not commit adultery:

But I say unto you, That whosoever looketh on a woman to lust after her hath committed adultery with her already in his heart.

Matthew 5:27,28

And He said, That which cometh out of the man, that defileth the man.

For from within, out of the heart of men, proceed evil thoughts, adulteries, fornications, murders,

Thefts, covetousness, wickedness, deceit, lasciviousness, an evil eye, blasphemy, pride, foolishness:

All these evil things come from within, and defile the man.

Mark 7:20-23

Flee fornication. Every sin that a man doeth is without the body; but he

that committeth fornication sinneth
against his own body.
1 Corinthians 6:18

And the peace of God, which
passeth all understanding, shall keep
your hearts and minds through Christ
Jesus.
Finally, brethren, whatsoever
things are true, whatsoever things are
honest, whatsoever things are just,
whatsoever things are pure, whatsoever
things are lovely, whatsoever things are
of good report; if there be any virtue,
and if there be any praise, think on
these things. *Philippians 4:7,8*

Abstain from all appearance of
evil. *1 Thessalonians 5:22*

Flee also youthful lusts: but follow
righteousness, faith, charity, peace,
with them that call on the Lord out of a
pure heart. *2 Timothy 2:22*

Submit yourselves therefore to
God. Resist the devil, and he will flee
from you. *James 4:7*

88

WHEN YOU ARE TEMPTED TO RETALIATE AGAINST ADVERSARIES

Blessed is the man that walketh not in the counsel of the ungodly, nor standeth in the way of sinners, nor sitteth in the seat of the scornful.

Psalm 1:1

I will both lay me down in peace, and sleep: for Thou, Lord, only makest me dwell in safety.   *Psalm 4:8*

Delight thyself also in the Lord: and He shall give thee the desires of thine heart.

Commit thy way unto the Lord; trust also in Him; and He shall bring it pass.

Rest in the Lord, and wait patiently for Him: fret not thyself because of him who prospereth in his way, because of the man who bringeth wicked devices to pass.

Cease from anger, and forsake wrath: fret not thyself in any wise to do evil.   *Psalm 37:4,5,7,8*

But the fruit of the Spirit is love, joy, peace, longsuffering, gentleness, goodness, faith,

Meekness, temperance: against such there is no law.

And they that are Christ's have crucified the flesh with the affections and lusts.   *Galatians 5:22-24*

Be ye angry, and sin not: let not the sun go down upon your wrath:
                              Ephesians 4:26

Do all things without murmurings and disputings: *Philippians 2:14*

But now ye also put off all these; anger, wrath, malice, blasphemy, filthy communication out of your mouth.

Lie not one to another, seeing that ye have put off the old man with his deeds;   *Colossians 3:8,9*

I will therefore that men pray every where, lifting up holy hands, without wrath and doubting.
1 Timothy 2:8

Wherefore, my beloved brethren, let every man be swift to hear, slow to speak, slow to wrath:

For the wrath of man worketh not the righteousness of God.

Wherefore lay apart all filthiness and superfluity of naughtiness, and receive with meekness the engrafted word, which is able to save your souls.
James 1:19-21

But if ye have bitter envying and strife in your hearts, glory not, and lie not against the truth.

This wisdom descendeth not from above, but is earthly, sensual, devilish.

For where envying and strife is, there is confusion and every evil work.
James 3:14-16

❧ 89 ❧

WHEN YOU ARE DISAPPOINTED WITH CHURCH MEMBERS

And the Lord said unto him, Who hath made man's mouth? or who maketh the dumb, or deaf, or the seeing, or the blind? have not I the Lord?

Now therefore go, and I will be with thy mouth, and teach thee what thou shalt say.   *Exodus 4:11,12*

That which I see not teach Thou me: if I have done iniquity, I will do no more.   *Job 34:32*

Lead me, O Lord, in Thy righteousness because of mine enemies; make Thy way straight before my face.

Psalm 5:8

I will bless the Lord, Who hath given me counsel: my reins also instruct me in the night seasons.

Psalm 16:7

I will instruct thee and teach thee in the way which thou shalt go: I will guide thee with Mine eye.   *Psalm 32:8*

It is better to trust in the Lord than to put confidence in man.
It is better to trust in the Lord than to put confidence in princes.

Psalm 118:8,9

But when they shall lead you, and deliver you up, take no thought beforehand what ye shall speak, neither do ye premeditate: but whatsoever shall be given you in that hour, that speak ye: for it is not ye that speak, but the Holy Ghost.   *Mark 13:11*

Howbeit when He, the Spirit of truth, is come, He will guide you into all truth: for He shall not speak of Himself; but whatsoever He shall hear, that shall He speak: and He will shew you things to come.   *John 16:13*

Those Who Created
    The Pain Of Yesterday
Do Not Control
    The Pleasure Of Tomorrow.

-MIKE MURDOCK

❧ 90 ❧

WHEN YOU ARE TEMPTED TO HOLD A GRUDGE

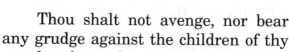

Thou shalt not avenge, nor bear any grudge against the children of thy people, but thou shalt love thy neighbour as thyself: I am the Lord.

Levitcus 19:18

The discretion of a man deferreth his anger; and it is his glory to pass over a transgression.   *Proverbs 19:11*

Rejoice not when thine enemy falleth, and let not thine heart be glad when he stumbleth:

Say not, I will do so to him as he hath done to me: I will render to the man according to his work.

Proverbs 24:17,29

If thine enemy be hungry, give him bread to eat; and if he be thirsty, give him water to drink:

For thou shalt heap coals of fire upon his head, and the Lord shall reward thee.   *Proverbs 25:21,22*

Also take no heed unto all words that are spoken; lest thou hear thy servant curse thee: *Ecclesiastes 7:21*

Blessed are the merciful: for they shall obtain mercy.

But I say unto you, That ye resist not evil: but whosoever shall smite thee on thy right cheek, turn to him the other also.

But I say unto you, Love your enemies, bless them that curse you, do good to them that hate you, and pray for them which despitefully use you, and persecute you;

For if ye love them which love you, what reward have ye? do not even the publicans the same?

Matthew 5:7,39,44,46

And forgive us our debts, as we

forgive our debtors.

For if ye forgive men their trespasses, your heavenly Father will also forgive you:

But if ye forgive not men their trespasses, neither will your Father forgive your trespasses.

Matthew 6:12,14,15

Then came Peter to Him, and said, Lord, how oft shall my brother sin against me, and I forgive him? till seven times?

Jesus saith unto him, I say not unto thee, Until seven times: but, Until seventy times seven. *Matthew 18:21,22*

And when ye stand praying, forgive, if ye have ought against any: that your Father also which is in heaven may forgive you your trespasses. *Mark 11:25*

And be ye kind one to another, tenderhearted, forgiving one another, even as God for Christ's sake hath forgiven you. *Ephesians 4:32*

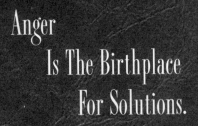

Anger
Is The Birthplace
For Solutions.

-MIKE MURDOCK

✨ 91 ✨

WHEN YOU FEEL
INFERIOR TO THOSE
MORE SUCCESSFUL

━━━━➤◦◦◦◦◦━━━━

Seek the Lord and His strength, seek His face continually.

1 Chronicles 16:11

The righteous also shall hold on his way, and he that hath clean hands shall be stronger and stronger. *Job 17:9*

Though he fall, he shall not be utterly cast down: for the Lord upholdeth him with His hand.

Psalm 37:24

The Lord will perfect that which concerneth me: Thy mercy, O Lord, endureth for ever: forsake not the works of Thine own hands. *Psalm 138:8*

But the path of the just is as the shining light, that shineth more and more unto the perfect day.

Proverbs 4:18

Therefore turn thou to thy God: keep mercy and judgment, and wait on thy God continually.   *Hosea 12:6*

But he that shall endure unto the end, the same shall be saved.

Matthew 24:13

And the Lord said, Simon, Simon, behold, satan hath desired to have you, that he may sift you as wheat:

But I have prayed for thee, that thy faith fail not: and when thou art converted, strengthen thy brethren.

Luke 22:31,32

Be sober, be vigilant; because your adversary the devil, as a roaring lion, walketh about, seeking whom he may devour: *1 Peter 5:8*

❧ 92 ❧

WHEN YOU FEEL ENVIOUS

For wrath killeth the foolish man, and envy slayeth the silly one.

I have seen the foolish taking root: but suddenly I cursed his habitation.

Job 5:2,3

Fret not thyself because of evildoers, neither be thou envious against the workers of iniquity.

Rest in the Lord, and wait patiently for Him: fret not thyself because of him who prospereth in his way, because of the man who bringeth wicked devices to pass.   *Psalm 37:1,7*

Be not thou afraid when one is made rich, when the glory of his house is increased;   *Psalm 49:16*

For I was envious at the foolish,

when I saw the prosperity of the wicked. *Psalm 73:3*

The wicked shall see it, and be grieved; he shall gnash with his teeth, and melt away: the desire of the wicked shall perish. *Psalm 112:10*

Envy thou not the oppressor, and choose none of his ways. *Proverbs 3:31*

A sound heart is the life of the flesh: but envy the rottenness of the bones. *Proverbs 14:30*

Let not thine heart envy sinners: but be thou in the fear of the Lord all the day long. *Proverbs 23:17*

Be not thou envious against evil men, neither desire to be with them.
Proverbs 24:1

Wrath is cruel, and anger is outrageous; but who is able to stand before envy? *Proverbs 27:4*

Hear ye, and give ear; be not

proud: for the Lord hath spoken.

Jeremiah 13:15

And such were some of you: but ye are washed, but ye are sanctified, but ye are justified in the name of the Lord Jesus, and by the Spirit of our God.

1 Corinthians 6:11

Envyings, murders, drunkenness, revellings, and such like: of the which I tell you before, as I have also told you in time past, that they which do such things shall not inherit the kingdom of God.

Let us not be desirous of vain glory, provoking one another, envying one another.   *Galatians 5:21,26*

He is proud, knowing nothing, but doting about questions and strifes of words, whereof cometh envy, strife, railings, evil surmisings,

Perverse disputings of men of corrupt minds, and destitute of the truth, supposing that gain is godliness: from such withdraw thyself.

1 Timothy 6:4,5

For we ourselves also were sometimes foolish, disobedient, deceived, serving divers lusts and pleasures, living in malice and envy, hateful, and hating one another.

Titus 3:3

But if ye have bitter envying and strife in your hearts, glory not, and lie not against the truth.

This wisdom descendeth not from above, but is earthly, sensual, devilish.

For where envying and strife is, there is confusion and every evil work.

James 3:14-16

Do ye think that the scripture saith in vain, The spirit that dwelleth in us lusteth to envy?   *James 4:5*

Grudge not one against another, brethren, lest ye be condemned: behold, the judge standeth before the door.

James 5:9

Wherefore laying aside all malice, and all guile, and hypocrisies, and envies, and all evil speakings,

1 Peter 2:1

93

WHEN YOU FEEL REJECTED

Trust in the Lord, and do good; so shalt thou dwell in the land, and verily thou shalt be fed.

Delight thyself also in the Lord; and He shall give thee the desires of thine heart.

Commit thy way unto the Lord; trust also in Him; and He shall bring it to pass.

And He shall bring forth thy righteousness as the light, and thy judgment as the noonday.

Rest in the Lord, and wait patiently for Him: fret not thyself because of him who prospereth in his way, because of the man who bringeth wicked devices to pass.

Cease from anger, and forsake

wrath: fret not thyself in any wise to do evil.

For evildoers shall be cut off: but those that wait upon the Lord, they shall inherit the earth.   *Psalm 37:3-9*

He that is slow to anger is better than the mighty; and he that ruleth his spirit than he that taketh a city.
Proverbs 16:32

The discretion of a man deferreth his anger; and it is his glory to pass over a transgression.   *Proverbs 19:11*

Charity suffereth long, and is kind; charity envieth not; charity vaunteth not itself, is not puffed up,

Doth not behave itself unseemly, seeketh not her own, is not easily provoked, thinketh no evil;
1 Corinthians 13:4,5

And let us not be weary in well doing: for in due season we shall reap, if we faint not.   *Galatians 6:9*

Be careful for nothing; but in every thing by prayer and supplication with thanksgiving let your requests be made known unto God.

And the peace of God, which passeth all understanding, shall keep your hearts and minds through Christ Jesus.

Finally, brethren, whatsoever things are true, whatsoever things are honest, whatsoever things are just, whatsoever things are pure, whatsoever things are lovely, whatsoever things are of good report; if there be any virtue, and if there be any praise, think on these things.   *Philippians 4:6-8*

Wherefore, my beloved brethren, let every man be swift to hear, slow to speak, slow to wrath: *James 1:19*

For this is thankworthy, if a man for conscience toward God endure grief, suffering wrongfully.   *1 Peter 2:19*

～ 94 ～

WHEN YOU FEEL BETRAYED

And David went out to meet them, and answered and said unto them, If ye be come peaceably unto me to help me, mine heart shall be knit unto you: but if ye be come to betray me to mine enemies, seeing there is no wrong in mine hands, the God of our fathers look thereon, and rebuke it.

1 Chronicles 12:17

False witnesses did rise up; they laid to my charge things that I knew not.

They rewarded me evil for good to the spoiling of my soul.

But as for me, when they were sick, my clothing was sackcloth: I humbled my soul with fasting; and my prayer returned into mine own bosom.

I behaved myself as though he had been my friend or brother: I bowed down heavily, as one that mourneth for his mother.

But in mine adversity they rejoiced, and gathered themselves together: yea, the abjects gathered themselves together against me, and I knew it not; they did tear me, and ceased not:

Lord, how long wilt Thou look on? rescue my soul from their destructions, my darling from the lions.

Psalm 35:11-15,17

Judge not, and ye shall not be judged: condemn not, and ye shall not be condemned: forgive, and ye shall be forgiven: *Luke 6:37*

Take heed to yourselves: If thy brother trespass against thee, rebuke him; and if he repent, forgive him.

And if he trespass against thee seven times in a day, and seven times in a day turn again to thee, saying, I repent; thou shalt forgive him.

Luke 17:3,4

And be ye kind one to another, tenderhearted, forgiving one another, even as God for Christ's sake hath forgiven you. *Ephesians 4:32*

For he that will love life, and see good days, let him refrain his tongue from evil, and his lips that they speak no guile:

Let him eschew evil, and do good; let him seek peace, and ensue it.

1 Peter 3:10,11

❧ 95 ❧

WHEN YOU WORRY
ABOUT RETIREMENT

Have not I commanded thee? Be strong and of a good courage; be not afraid, neither be thou dismayed: for the Lord thy God is with thee whithersoever thou goest.   *Joshua 1:9*

Be not afraid nor dismayed by reason of this great multitude; for the battle is not yours, but God's.

Believe in the Lord your God, so shall ye be established; believe His prophets, so shall ye prosper.

2 Chronicles 20:15,20

For they all made us afraid, saying, Their hands shall be weakened from the work, that it be not done. Now therefore, O God, strengthen my hands.

Nehemiah 6:9

In famine He shall redeem thee from death: and in war from the power of the sword.

At destruction and famine thou shalt laugh: neither shalt thou be afraid of the beasts of the earth. *Job 5:20,22*

Commit thy way unto the Lord; trust also in Him; and He shall bring it to pass.

I have been young, and now am old; yet have I not seen the righteous forsaken, nor his seed begging bread.
Psalm 37:5,25

Cast thy burden upon the Lord, and He shall sustain thee: He shall never suffer the righteous to be moved.
Psalm 55:22

It is better to trust in the Lord than to put confidence in man.
Psalm 118:8

Trust in the Lord with all thine heart; and lean not unto thine own understanding. *Proverbs 3:5*

Commit thy works unto the Lord, and thy thoughts shall be established.
Proverbs 16:3

The fear of man bringeth a snare: but whoso putteth his trust in the Lord shall be safe. *Proverbs 29:25*

Blessed is the man that trusteth in the Lord, and whose hope the Lord is.

For he shall be as a tree planted by the waters, and that spreadeth out her roots by the river, and shall not see when heat cometh, but her leaf shall be green; and shall not be careful in the year of drought, neither shall cease from yielding fruit. *Jeremiah 17:7,8*

Be not ye therefore like unto them: for your Father knoweth what things ye have need of, before ye ask Him.

Behold the fowls of the air: for they sow not, neither do they reap, nor gather into barns; yet your heavenly Father feedeth them. Are ye not much better than they?

Wherefore, if God so clothe the

grass of the field, which to day is, and to morrow is cast into the oven, shall He not much more clothe you, O ye of little faith?

Therefore take no thought, saying, What shall we eat? or, What shall we drink? or, Wherewithal shall we be clothed?

But seek ye first the kingdom of God, and His righteousness; and all these things shall be added unto you.

Matthew 6:8,26,30,31,33

Jesus said unto him, If thou canst believe, all things are possible to him that believeth. *Mark 9:23*

I have fought a good fight, I have finished my course, I have kept the faith:

Henceforth there is laid up for me a crown of righteousness, which the Lord, the righteous judge, shall give me at that day: and not to me only, but unto all them also that love His appearing. *2 Timothy 4:7,8*

∼ 96 ∼

WHEN YOU LOSE CONFIDENCE IN YOUR PREACHING ABILITY

Now therefore go, and I will be with thy mouth, and teach thee what thou shalt say.   *Exodus 4:12*

Who can understand his errors? cleanse Thou me from secret faults.
                               Psalm 19:12

It is better to hear the rebuke of the wise, than for a man to hear the song of fools.   *Ecclesiastes 7:5*

But they that wait upon the Lord shall renew their strength; they shall mount up with wings as eagles; they shall run, and not be weary; and they shall walk, and not faint.   *Isaiah 40:31*

For the Holy Ghost shall teach you in the same hour what ye ought to say.
Luke 12:12

Now when they saw the boldness of Peter and John, and perceived that they were unlearned and ignorant men, they marvelled; and they took knowledge of them, that they had been with Jesus.

And now, Lord, behold their threatenings: and grant unto Thy servants, that with all boldness they may speak Thy word,   *Acts 4:13,29*

And I, brethren, when I came to you, came not with excellency of speech or of wisdom, declaring unto you the testimony of God.

And my speech and my preaching was not with enticing words of man's wisdom, but in demonstration of the Spirit and of power:

That your faith should not stand in the wisdom of men, but in the power of God.   *1 Corinthians 2;1,4,5*

For we walk by faith, not by sight:
2 Corinthians 5:7

For God hath not given us the spirit of fear; but of power, and of love, and of a sound mind. *2 Timothy 1:7*

Notwithstanding the Lord stood with me, and strengthened me; that by me the preaching might be fully known, and that all the Gentiles might hear: and I was delivered out of the mouth of the lion. *2 Timothy 4:17*

And for me, that utterance may be given unto me, that I may open my mouth boldly, to make known the mystery of the gospel, *Ephesians 6:19*

If any of you lack wisdom, let him ask of God, that giveth to all men liberally, and upbraideth not; and it shall be given him. *James 1:5*

But ye, beloved, building up yourselves on your most holy faith, praying in the holy Ghost, *Jude 1:20*

❧ 97 ❧

WHEN YOU LOSE CONFIDENCE IN YOUR LEADERSHIP SKILLS

Who can understand his errors? cleanse Thou me from secret faults.
Psalm 19:12

Trust in the Lord with all thine heart; and lean not unto thine own understanding.　　*Proverbs 3:5*

For the Lord God will help me; therefore shall I not be confounded: therefore have I set my face like a flint, and I know that I shall not be ashamed.
Isaiah 50:7

For I will give you a mouth and wisdom, which all your adversaries shall not be able to gainsay nor resist.
Luke 21:15

But ye shall receive power, after that the Holy Ghost is come upon you: and ye shall be witnesses unto Me both in Jerusalem, and in all Judaea, and in Samaria, and unto the uttermost part of the earth.   *Acts 1:8*

Let us therefore come boldly unto the throne of grace, that we may obtain mercy, and find grace to help in time of need.   *Hebrews 4:16*

If any of you lack wisdom, let him ask of God, that giveth to all men liberally, and upbraideth not; and it shall be given him.   *James 1:5*

Take, my brethren, the prophets, who have spoken in the name of the Lord, for an example of suffering affliction, and of patience.   *James 5:10*

For it is better, if the will of God be so, that ye suffer for well doing, than for evil doing.   *1 Peter 3:17*

But ye have an unction from the Holy One, and ye know all things.
                    1 John 2:20

98

WHEN YOU LOSE THE DESIRE TO LEARN

Lead me in Thy truth, and teach me: for Thou art the God of my salvation; on Thee do I wait all the day.
Psalm 25:5

Hear, ye children, the instruction of a father, and attend to know understanding.
Proverbs 4:1

Hear instruction, and be wise, and refuse it not.
Proverbs 8:33

But the comforter, which is the Holy Ghost, Whom the Father will send in My name, He shall teach you all things, and bring all things to your remembrance, whatsoever I have said unto you.
John 14:26

Till I come, give attendance to reading, to exhortation, to doctrine.

Meditate upon these things; give thyself wholly to them; that thy profiting may appear to all.

1 Timothy 4:13,15

Study to shew thyself approved unto God, a workman that needeth not to be ashamed, rightly dividing the word of truth. *2 Timothy 2:15*

If any of you lack wisdom, let him ask of God, that giveth to all men liberally, and upbraideth not; and it shall be given him. *James 1:5*

According as His divine power hath given unto us all things that pertain unto life and godliness, through the knowledge of Him that hath called us to glory and virtue: *2 Peter 1:3*

If any man have an ear, let him hear. *Revelation 13:9*

❧ 99 ❧

WHEN YOU FEEL WITHDRAWN AND DISTANCED IN FELLOWSHIPPING WITH OTHER MINISTERS

————◆━◦━◆————

Then they that feared the Lord spake often one to another: and the Lord hearkened, and heard it, and a book of remembrance was written before Him for them that feared the Lord, and that thought upon His name.
Malachi 3:16

For every one that asketh receiveth; and he that seeketh findeth; and to him that knocketh it shall be opened.
Matthew 7:8

Moreover if thy brother shall

trespass against thee, go and tell him his fault between thee and him alone: if he shall hear thee, thou has gained thy brother.   *Matthew 18:15*

The Spirit of the Lord is upon Me, because He hath anointed Me to preach the gospel to the poor; He hath sent Me to heal the brokenhearted, to preach deliverance to the captives, and recovering of sight to the blind, to set at liberty them that are bruised,
Luke 4:18

And let us consider one another to provoke unto love and to good works:

Not forsaking the assembling of ourselves together, as the manner of some is; but exhorting one another: and so much the more, as ye see the day approaching.   *Hebrews 10:24,25*

Remember them which have the rule over you, who have spoken unto you the word of God: whose faith follow, considering the end of their conversation.   *Hebrews 13:7*

YOUR MENTORS AND PROTÉGÉS

∾ 100 ∾

WHEN YOU LOSE CONFIDENCE IN YOUR MENTOR

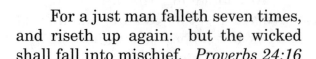

For a just man falleth seven times, and riseth up again: but the wicked shall fall into mischief. *Proverbs 24:16*

Who art thou that judgest another man's servant? to his own master he standeth or falleth. Yea, he shall be holden up: for God is able to make him stand.

I know, and am persuaded by the

Lord Jesus, that there is nothing unclean of itself: but to him that esteemeth any thing to be unclean, to him it is unclean. *Romans 14:4,10*

Brethren, if a man be overtaken in a fault, ye which are spiritual, restore such an one in the spirit of meekness; considering thyself, lest thou also be tempted.

But let every man prove his own work, and then shall he have rejoicing in himself alone, and not in another.

Galatians 6:1,4

I therefore, the prisoner of the Lord, beseech you that ye walk worthy of the vocation wherewith ye are called,

With all lowliness and meekness, with longsuffering, forbearing one another in love;

Endeavouring to keep the unity of the Spirit in the bond of peace.

Ephesians 4:1-3

Forbearing one another, and forgiving one another, if any man have

a quarrel against any: even as Christ
forgave you, so also do ye.

Colossians 3:13

Rebuke not an elder, but intreat
him as a father; and the younger men
as brethren;   *1 Timothy 5:1*

Remember them which have the
rule over you, who have spoken unto
you the word of God: whose faith follow,
considering the end of their conversation.

Hebrews 13:7

❧ 101 ❧

WHEN YOUR MENTOR FAILS TO SHOW TRUE CARING FOR YOUR GOALS

My son, despise not the chastening of the Lord; neither be weary of His correction.

For whom the Lord loveth He correcteth; even as a father the son in whom he delighteth.

For the Lord shall be thy confidence, and shall keep thy foot from being taken.   *Proverbs 3:11,12,26*

For the Lord God will help me; therefore shall I not be confounded: therefore have I set my face like a flint, and I know that I shall not be ashamed.
Isaiah 50:7

What shall we then say to these things? If God be for us, who can be against us?   *Romans 8:31*

I beseech Euodias, and beseech Syntyche, that they be of the same mind in the Lord.   *Philippians 4:12*

Forbearing one another, and forgiving one another, if any man have a quarrel against any: even as Christ forgave you, so also do ye.
Colossians 3:13

Rebuke not an elder, but intreat him as a father; and the younger men as brethren;   *1 Timothy 5:1*

For consider him that endured such contradiction of sinners against himself, lest ye be wearied and faint in your minds.   *Hebrews 12:3*

Knowing this, that the trying of your faith worketh patience. *James 1:3*

❧ 102 ❧

WHEN YOU LOSE PASSION IN MENTORING YOUR PROTÉGÉS

———◆❖◆———

Be ye strong therefore, and let not your hands be weak: for your work shall be rewarded.   *2 Chronicles 15:7*

I will stand upon my watch, and set me upon the tower, and will watch to see what he will say unto me, and what I shall answer when I am reproved.

For the vision is yet for an appointed time, but at the end it shall speak, and not lie: though it tarry, wait for it; because it will surely come, it will not tarry.   *Habakkuk 2:1,3*

We then that are strong ought to

bear the infirmities of the weak, and not to please ourselves.

Now the God of patience and consolation grant you to be likeminded one toward another according to Christ Jesus: *Romans 15:1,5*

For though I preach the gospel, I have nothing to glory of: for necessity is laid upon me; yea, woe is unto me, if I preach not the gospel!

And this I do for the gospel's sake, that I might be partaker thereof with you.

Know ye not that they which run in a race run all, but one receiveth the prize? So run, that ye may obtain.

And every man that striveth for the mastery is temperate in all things. Now they do it to obtain a corruptible crown; but we an incorruptible.

1 Corinthians 9:16,23-25

Ye did run well; who did hinder you that ye should not obey the truth?

A little leaven leaveneth the whole lump.   *Galatians 5:7,9*

Let him that is taught in the word communicate unto him that teacheth in all good things.

And let us not be weary in well doing: for in due season we shall reap, if we faint not.

As we have therefore opportunity, let us do good unto all men, especially unto them who are of the household of faith. *Galatians 6:6,9,10*

I have fought a good fight, I have finished my course, I have kept the faith: *2 Timothy 4:7*

Knowing this, that the trying of your faith worketh patience. *James 1:3*

≈ 103 ≈

WHEN YOU LOSE CONFIDENCE IN THE CHARACTER OF YOUR PROTÉGÉS

Moreover as for me, God forbid that I should sin against the Lord in ceasing to pray for you: but I will teach you the good and the right way:

1 Samuel 12:23

For by wise counsel thou shalt make thy war: and in multitude of counsellors there is safety.

Proverbs 24:6

Two are better than one; because they have a good reward for their labour.

For if they fall, the one will lift up his fellow: bur woe to him that is alone when he falleth; for he hath not another to help him up.   *Ecclesiastes 4:9,10*

But I have prayed for thee, that thy faith fail not: and when thou art converted, strengthen thy brethren.
Luke 22:32

Therefore watch, and remember, that by the space of three years I ceased not to warn every one night and day with tears.

And now, brethren, I commend you to God, and to the word of His grace, which is able to build you up, and to give you an inheritance among all them which are sanctified.   *Acts 20:31,32*

But if thy brother be grieved with thy meat, now walkest thou not charitably. Destroy not him with thy meat, for whom Christ died.
Romans 14:15

For Demas hath forsaken me, having loved this present world, and is departed unto Thessalonica; Crescens to Galatia, Titus unto Dalmatia.
2 Timothy 4:10

❧ 104 ❧

WHEN YOU LOSE PATIENCE WITH YOUR PROTÉGÉS

━━━━●◦◦●━━━━

My lips shall not speak wickedness, nor my tongue utter deceit.
Job 27:4

He that is slow to wrath is of great understanding: but he that is hasty of spirit exalteth folly. *Proverbs 14:29*

The disciple is not above his master, nor the servant above his lord.

It is enough for the disciple that he be as his master, and the servant as his lord. If they have called the master of the house Beelzebub, how much more shall they call them of his household?

Fear them not therefore: for there is nothing covered, that shall not be revealed; and hid, that shall not be known. *Matthew 10:24-26*

Forbearing one another, and forgiving one another, if any man have a quarrel against any: even as Christ forgave you, so also do ye.
Colossians 3:13

Now we exhort you, brethren, warn them that are unruly, comfort the feebleminded, support the weak, be patient toward all men.
1 Thessalonians 5:14

Wherefore seeing we also are compassed about with so great a cloud of witnesses, let us lay aside every weight, and the sin which doth so easily beset us, and let us run with patience the race that is set before us,

Looking unto Jesus the author and finisher of our faith; who for the joy that was set before Him endured the cross, despising the shame, and is set down at the right hand of the throne of God.

For consider Him that endured

such contradiction of sinners against Himself, lest ye be wearied and faint in your minds.

Ye have not yet resisted unto blood, striving against sin.

Hebrews 12:1-4

Knowing this, that the trying of your faith worketh patience.

But let patience have her perfect work, that ye may be perfect and entire, wanting nothing.   *James 1:3,4*

Wherefore laying aside all malice, and all guile, and hypocrisies, and envies, and all evil speakings,

1 Peter 2:1

☙ 105 ❧

WHEN YOUR PROTÉGÉS WANT SPONSORSHIP INSTEAD OF MENTORSHIP

Behold, happy is the man whom God correcteth: therefore despise not thou the chastening of the Almighty:
Job 5:17

He that rebuketh a man afterwards shall find more favour than he that flattereth with the tongue.
Proverbs 28:23

Correct thy son, and he shall give thee rest; yea, he shall give delight unto thy soul.   *Proverbs 29:17*

For every one shall be salted with fire, and every sacrifice shall be salted with salt.

Salt is good: but if the salt have lost his saltness, wherewith will ye season it? Have salt in yourselves, and have peace one with another.

Mark 9:49,50

Therefore watch, and remember, that by the space of three years I ceased not to warn every one night and day with tears. *Acts 20:31*

Let your speech be alway with grace, seasoned with salt, that ye may know how ye ought to answer every man. *Colossians 4:6*

And the servant of the Lord must not strive; but be gentle unto all men, apt to teach, patient,

In meekness instructing those that oppose themselves; if God peradventure will give them repentance to the acknowledging of the truth;

And that they may recover themselves out of the snare of the devil, who are taken captive by him at his will.   *2 Timothy 2:24-26*

Put them in mind to be subject to principalities and powers, to obey magistrates, to be ready to every good work,

To speak evil of no man, to be no brawlers, but gentle, shewing all meekness unto all men.

For we ourselves also were sometimes foolish, disobedient, deceived, serving divers lusts and pleasures, living in malice and envy, hateful, and hating one another.

Titus 3:1-3

Knowing this, that the trying of your faith worketh patience. *James 1:3*

2004

January
S	M	T	W	T	F	S
				1	2	3
4	5	6	7	8	9	10
11	12	13	14	15	16	17
18	19	20	21	22	23	24
25	26	27	28	29	30	31

February
S	M	T	W	T	F	S
1	2	3	4	5	6	7
8	9	10	11	12	13	14
15	16	17	18	19	20	21
22	23	24	25	26	27	28
29						

March
S	M	T	W	T	F	S
	1	2	3	4	5	6
7	8	9	10	11	12	13
14	15	16	17	18	19	20
21	22	23	24	25	26	27
28	29	30	31			

April
S	M	T	W	T	F	S
				1	2	3
4	5	6	7	8	9	10
11	12	13	14	15	16	17
18	19	20	21	22	23	24
25	26	27	28	29	30	

May
S	M	T	W	T	F	S
						1
2	3	4	5	6	7	8
9	10	11	12	13	14	15
16	17	18	19	20	21	22
23	24	25	26	27	28	29
30	31					

June
S	M	T	W	T	F	S
		1	2	3	4	5
6	7	8	9	10	11	12
13	14	15	16	17	18	19
20	21	22	23	24	25	26
27	28	29	30			

July
S	M	T	W	T	F	S
				1	2	3
4	5	6	7	8	9	10
11	12	13	14	15	16	17
18	19	20	21	22	23	24
25	26	27	28	29	30	31

August
S	M	T	W	T	F	S
1	2	3	4	5	6	7
8	9	10	11	12	13	14
15	16	17	18	19	20	21
22	23	24	25	26	27	28
29	30	31				

September
S	M	T	W	T	F	S
			1	2	3	4
5	6	7	8	9	10	11
12	13	14	15	16	17	18
19	20	21	22	23	24	25
26	27	28	29	30		

October
S	M	T	W	T	F	S
					1	2
3	4	5	6	7	8	9
10	11	12	13	14	15	16
17	18	19	20	21	22	23
24	25	26	27	28	29	30
31						

November
S	M	T	W	T	F	S
	1	2	3	4	5	6
7	8	9	10	11	12	13
14	15	16	17	18	19	20
21	22	23	24	25	26	27
28	29	30				

December
S	M	T	W	T	F	S
			1	2	3	4
5	6	7	8	9	10	11
12	13	14	15	16	17	18
19	20	21	22	23	24	25
26	27	28	29	30	31	

ABOUT *MIKE MURDOCK*

- Has embraced his Assignment to pursue...possess...and publish the Wisdom of God to help people achieve their dreams and goals.

- Began full-time evangelism at the age of 19, which has continued since 1966.

- Has traveled and spoken to more than 14,000 audiences in 38 countries, including East and West Africa, the Orient and Europe.

- Noted author of over 140 books, including best sellers, *"Wisdom For Winning," "Dream Seeds"* and *"The Double Diamond Principle."*

- Created the popular *"Topical Bible"* series for Businessmen, Mothers, Fathers, Teenagers, and the *"One- Minute Pocket Bible"* series and *"The Uncommon Life"* series.

- Has composed more than 5,700 songs such as *"I Am Blessed," "You Can Make It," "Holy Spirit This Is Your House"* and *"Jesus, Just The Mention Of Your Name,"* recorded by many gospel artists.

- Is the Founder of The Wisdom Center, in Denton Texas.

- Has a weekly television program called *"Wisdom Keys With Mike Murdock."*

- Has appeared often on TBN, CBN, BET and other television network programs.

- Is a Founding Trustee on the Board of Charismatic Bible Ministries with Oral Roberts.

- Has had more than 3,500 accept the call into full-time ministry under his ministry.